ISBN: 978-1-68092-081-9
Published by Jamel Jackson
© 2017 Jamel Jackson

*To Tatia*

# THE VALUE OF RELATIONSHIPS

*May Gods grace + mercy continue to cover you and your family*

*Dream Big*

## JAMEL JACKSON

# Index

# Dedication

There is no way I could consolidate the value of relationships into one word, one sentence, one paragraph or even one book. I believe this is an eternal book that will exist long after I'm gone. There are so many individuals who have inspired me to push beyond my limits. I would like to dedicate this book to:

First and foremost Jesus Christ and all the Kingdom sons & daughters.

My wife Jacquelyn Jackson for standing by my side through every obstacle.

My son Nehemiah and daughter Jireh Jackson, every conversation with you guys inspires me in so many ways.

My Mom and Dad for giving me your best and continuing to encourage me. I love you both beyond words.

My brother Terrance Jackson & Eraina Jackson Rest with the King, my brother Cassius Jackson, my brother DJ Fadelf for being a big brother when I needed someone to share my personal thoughts with, and my sister Racheal Jackson I love you big head.

David Shands for not taking no for an answer and provoking me to write when I wanted to sleep.

Pastor Anthony Wallace for the message you delivered on the 1st Sunday in November 2007. You stated that "If you submit vision to another vision and then it will come to pass, if you say what I say, you will have what I have because I'm only saying what my father says and he's only saying what the Father is saying."

Pastor Ashley and Jane Evans - the brief time that we have know each other has impacted and propelled my life to another level.

Pastor Hart Ramsey - you're a prolific teacher.

Ray and Annette Cooper, Anthony Morris, Gary and Nicole Kennedy, Uriah Austin, Vickie Austin, Mom Austin, Reggie Goldsboro, Ty Fontaine, Pam Gallant, Jackie Tiller, Daniel Humprhies, Menno Chupp, Mr. Williams, Porschia Percell, Aunt Bosie, Momma Zdanczyk. I am so grateful for all you have invested in me. Onnaiese Epps for being one of the greatest friends I could ever ask for. Azhar, Regis and Worknesh Williams, it's been a pleasure to serve such a mighty man and women of God. Willie and Beth Hardmen, Earnest Davis, Chuck Mosely, Daniel and Jeneeh Gueh, Jerome and Tetra Shockely, Russel and Kiesha Burton, and Uncle PD.

# Introduction

There are many routes to having successful relationships. Many of us have chosen the route that leads to making ourselves happy and leaving the other person empty. Over the years, I have discovered the most valuable possession on this earth are relationships.

The dictionary defines valuable as a thing that is of great worth. Since the beginning of time, God has used relationships as the solution for every problem that exists. Ultimately, we have a choice to value or to devalue these relationships. There is definitely a process involved in developing a relationship with anyone. My wife and I have been together for eleven years, and we have been married ten and 1/2 years out of the eleven.

Now you better believe there have been days where I felt like throwing in the towel and giving up. This is where the forging of the relationship was solidified. This is where I had the option to value or to devalue the relationship. Trust, whatever you consider valuable will become top priority and whatever you devalue will become least priority. Relationships are always about prioritizing and organizing. Of course I chose to value my wife even when I didn't feel like it. If I had based my decision to value her on emotions then we would have had cubic zirconia marriage verses a marriage filled with gems and precious stones.

It was out of my marriage that I begin to look at all of my relationships with a new perspective. Even the way I looked at the creator was shifted. I had developed an entirely new value system. Now, I truly believe everything you need can be found inside of relationships.

First and foremost there needs to be a relationship established with the God who created you. Making him top priority has allowed me to see myself as high value and in return seeing everyone else as valuable. I am a firm believer that valuable people attract people of value. One of the most important things to remember is there is always going to be challenges which force you to step outside of your comfort zone in order to improve upon the relationship being created. In order to truly understand the value of relationship we need to return to the original blue print. I believe the Bible is filled with amazing stories of some of the greatest relationships that have ever existed on this planet.

The purpose of my book is to guide you on how to execute on the principles of relationships such as building a solid foundation, the priority of the process, forming agreements, communication, determining where you need to be versus where you want to be, and maintaining through it all. As you begin to navigate through the chapters of this book. I want you to keep these questions in mind. Who do you consider to be valuable in your life? Why do you consider him/her or them to be valuable? Do they add value to your life?

# Chapter 1 Building Blocks

In 2006, I remember my job as a contractor working for my friend Danny Humphries' construction company. Danny was responsible for building pole buildings and houses in the Delaware, Maryland, Virginia area. Danny was a brilliant young man who specialized in building houses and pole buildings. I remember watching him look over the blueprints of a project we were about to start. Most of the information on the blueprint looked like a mystical math equation until he begin to explain the drawings to me. Although I was ready, if the conditions of the soil were not ready there was nothing being built at all.

No matter how excited I was about building, there were many elements that factored into the process of starting. I'm not sure if you have ever built anything outside, but the climate plays an important role in each step of the plan. There would be days where we could not build due to inclement weather conditions. The most important part of the planning phase was establishing a solid foundation. This is what the entire house was going to built upon, and required the builder to be very meticulous. This phase required no room for foolishness from anyone who was involved.

Installing a foundation is not a simple one, two, three process, unless you are a highly-skilled contractor and even then you can run into issues. The most popular foundation used is a concrete slab because of it's durability and strength. On my first work site, each task seemed so tedious until I begin to walk through the steps. One of my jobs was clearing all large stones, debris and any disruptive objects that would prevent us from building correctly.

After laying several foundations God began to speak to me about my personal life. I remember him asking me "what are you building on"? I honestly had no answer at that time, except for "I don't know". In my heart I knew I was building every relationship on whatever I felt was solid for me. If the deal felt right it was concrete enough for me to move forward. Notice I said if the deal felt right. It didn't matter if the deal or relationship within the deal was going to take me off track, set me back, harm me, or potentially kill me. As long as it felt like it would be a great thing to do, I was all in. Thank God for his grace and him not allowing me to leap to far into to my folly.

One day, as I was researching the word foundation in the Bible I came across this scripture in the book of Matthew chapter 7 verse 24-27: <sup>24</sup>*Anyone who listens to my teaching and follows it is wise, like* *a person who builds a house on solid rock. <sup>25</sup>Though the rain comes in torrents and the floodwaters rise and the winds beat against that house, it won't collapse because it is built on bedrock. <sup>26</sup>But anyone who hears my teaching and doesn't obey it is foolish, like a person who builds a house on sand. <sup>27</sup>When the rains and floods come and the winds beat against that house, it will collapse with a mighty crash.*

After reading this passage I sat back on my bed. At the time, I was a newlywed and a father of two kids. I began to reflect back to building with Danny and how important it was to lay a solid foundation when building a house. He would tell me things like "Jackson - measure twice, cut once". Hey "Jackson you're smarter than the wood". Every intricate detail had to be precise, so I was constantly reminded to be conscientious of my decisions.

In life we tend to build relationships on whatever we deem to be fitting for the moment. We are not taking the time to pick a site and investigate the conditions of the soil. Like the scripture stated above - the rain, flood and winds are sure to come. Jesus did not say the rain, flood, and winds may come my people, He said they will come. It's in the torrents that we find out what we built the house on.

Remember there was a wise man and a foolish man. The fool said it's cool as long as he/she fine, as long as the company compensates me for my time this should surely last forever. I mean he/she did give me the best sex I have ever had, the company is paying me more money than I ever had. I know he/she cheats every now and then but the sex is the bomb and all my financial needs are met. I know the company I work for pours toxic waste into the cities' drinking water. I know the mission statement of the business goes against everything I stand for, but I have bills to pay.

These scenarios are not uncommon to me. I have spent countless hours speaking with couples, singles, and business owners. I have discovered that many of us have built our relationships on inadequate foundations from the beginning. Maybe you are someone who has already built a business, friendship, or marriage with the wrong tools. Maybe you are a teenager attempting to rekindle the relationship between your parents. Maybe you are the parents frustrated with your kids and wondering how are we going to reconnect with our kids.

One of the greatest things I love about my God is that he can redeem the time. Do not look at your failure of building on an inadequate foundation as a complete loss. You did the best you could with the information you had, and now it's time to rebuild. My objective in this book is to dismantle humanity's philosophy of independence from God and essentially each other. We need to get back to the original reason for our existence and determine which foundation is adequate and which one is inadequate. We also need to find exactly where we lost the value of relationship and make this the chief cornerstone of every relationship we establish from here on. Someone may ask; "well what if I do not believe in what you believe in?" It's perfectly fine if you do not believe in what I believe, that is what is so amazing about choice. Although we do not believe the same, I can assure you a large majority of the humans living on this planet believe in rain, floods and wind.

Every building, home, or relationship will face these weather conditions during some point in life. So ultimately, it will be more than a matter of approving or disproving a belief system. We all believe, but do we all accept what we believe. You can believe in something and not accept what comes with what you believe.

The young man decides to join the local gang in his city because his parents abandoned him at an early age. The gang has proven to give him more love than anyone and has even promised to protect him from any type of harm. The loyalty of the gang gives him a feeling of acceptance, security and self esteem, so he accepts everything that comes with what he believes. Even if what he believes in results in him being killed. So, he could have stopped at believing but the fact he accepted the gang as his new family and he accepted everything which came with the belief system.

As we can see, his entire foundation for family, love, and life was inadequate from the beginning. His parents probably had every intention on raising him to be a mature young man and perhaps even saw him as a straight-A student, graduating from one of the most prestigious schools. Unfortunately, who knows what their foundation or value system was built on.

Before we move forward, let me remind you that learning, knowing, and understanding your lineage gives you foundation, identity, and direction. It doesn't matter if you started building on an inadequate foundation, with the right adjustments your situation can reverse into the adequate position. Some buildings require a constant architectural examination. This is why revisiting the original blue print and understanding the mind of the maker is vital.

From the beginning God was letting us know the adequate material to build upon. As humans we have a choice and most of us choose our own prerogative. Adequate is defined as enough or satisfactory for a particular purpose. The purpose of mankind from the beginning was the value of relationship. It's in the beginning where we lose the value and choose to devalue what was given to us freely.

We must understand when two individuals value a relationship, they are not trying to get anything from each other as they are always trying to give. There are some of us who approach relationships with what I call a GETTO mentality. (I intentionally misspelled "ghetto" for illustration purposes.) These individuals are always looking to see what they can get.

Let's listen to the conversation where our value system shifted from give to get. I love the way the Bible translates the story. It says in Genesis chapter 3 verse 6: *⁶When the Woman saw that the tree looked like good eating and realized what she would get out of it-she'd know everything!-she took and ate the fruit and then gave some to her husband, and he ate.*

Now prior to this, the foundation for mankind was already set in place. There was a site picked out called Earth and everything man needed was at his disposal. There were no worries about murder, crime, forgiveness, trust, breached contracts, lack and no need for Jesus to physically run up on the scene - until the conversation in the garden took place. The Bible states that Eve looked at the tree, it looked good for eating and she realized what she would GET out of it. So here we see the first GET comes on the scene and the relationship between man and God is severed. We were completely cut out of having dominion and authority over the foundation. We lost the value in relationship with the main person relationship is suppose to start with.

Before anyone attempts to castigate the women for taking part in the enemy's deception, we need to remember Adam was chilling on the scene and didn't say anything, but he sure did partake in the foolishness. Now from that point forward we find this GET mentality erupting in every relationship.

There were two brothers named Cane and Able, where one decided to murder the other over something he could GET. This mentality continues to flow through generations until a King is born. He carried one purpose in mind which was to restore relationships. The majority of the world may believe in his method of restoration.

Once again it's not just a matter of believing it's also a matter of accepting so we can reap the benefits of the restoration. One of the greatest lessons I learned while valuing those God has placed in my life is that valuable people attract people of value. I have reached a point that even if a person devalues me, my purpose is still to value. In no way am I saying you become a doormat for people to walk on. Trust me, in the midst of you choosing to value, although it's not being reciprocated, you will develop a heart of gratitude, love, and giving. You will become so attractive that valuable people will come looking for you, simply because your foundation was built on something that is sufficient and supports purpose and longevity.

Once again I would like to reiterate and bring Mr. Matthew to the stand where he stated in the message translation of the Bible. Matthew chapter 7 verses 24-25: [24]*These words I speak to you are not incidental additions to your life, homeowner improvements to your standard of living. They are foundational words, words to build a life on. If you work these words into your life, you are like a smart carpenter who built his house on solid rock.* [25]*Rain poured down, the river flooded, a tornado hit- but nothing moved that house. It was fixed to the rock."*

The key word we see here is foundational. It's a word that is skimmed over in a microwave society. Relationships are rushed into dating without any direction or understanding of the importance of foundation. The young lady desires to be married but the young man doesn't feel he is prepared to marry. This does not make the young man selfish in any way. I actually commend his honesty. However, he's not willing to wait but acts as if he is married to the lady, by expecting her to perform like a wife. He desires some form of sexual activity but she desires to wait until marriage. He desires for her to have his children and cook, but the thought of marriage needs to be postponed. He says I really want to be married just not right now. I need to get to know you better before I make such a huge commitment. I believe if he's prepared to walk you in the bedroom he should be prepared to walk you down the aisle.

This particular illustration can be used to describe a man who is willing to wait and it's the female who is unwilling to yield. It's not a matter of waiting, but it's a matter of foundation. Remember the beginning stages are so vital. What you choose to build on, will determine the longevity of your structure. This structure applies to both business, family and male-female relationships. Ignoring the warning signs of a cracked foundation only leaves room for small concerns to become big headaches. These problems could ultimately cost a lot of money and time, and cause a lot of heartache. We need to put first things first by setting up boundaries that help us prioritize our lives. Sometimes the hardest thing to do is to say no in middle of a life-altering situation. Trust me, your "no" needs no explanation when it comes to laying the foundation for any of your relationships.

# SELF REFLECTION

## Chapter 2 Mutual Agreement

Amos chapter 3 verse 3 states: *Can two people walk together without agreeing on the direction?*

Whenever we decide to step into an agreement there will be some sort of compromise and commitment involved. They both have to exist in order for the agreement to be mutual. A person can be committed but not willing to compromise. Or a person can be willing to compromise but not be committed. The term "mutual" has to deal with a feeling or action experienced or accepted by two or more parties or people. This means that it doesn't matter if you agree or not. If I never agree with the direction, there is a strong possibility we will not reach our destination.

Moses, one of the great patriarchs of the Bible was given the assignment of setting his people free from the oppression of the Egyptians. Although Moses had a speaking problem, he did not let that keep him from coming into agreement with God's plan for his life and his people. Moses' agreement lead to a deep commitment and he was willing to compromise his own life for the sake of others. The commitment and the willingness to compromise his own safety gave him strength to face the Egyptian leader and boldly command him to let his people go.

You would think after setting them free, the people would have no reserve thoughts in their minds of going back to the brutality of living under oppression. Compromising involves settling a dispute between two people by mutual concession. To the former slaves, compromising was escaping the physical chains, unlawful labor and years of inflicted pain. It was finally being able to have freedom and take a lunch break whenever they wanted. The true fact is they settled the physical dispute but never settled the dispute in their minds and hearts. This is why they started out with a heart full of vigor committed to the journey to the promised land. As the journey through the desert started, the unsettling compromise in their hearts began to produce a complaining sound in the camp. After a few months into the journey, the promised land agreement wasn't mutual any longer.

After a few months of dating, sexting, late night talks and sweet-honey vocabulary, the love agreement wasn't mutual any longer. After a few years into the marriage the financial agreement wasn't mutual any longer. I find this story so interesting because not too long into the journey, the Israelites face some adversity reminding them of the harse conditions they were living under. Just the thought of them having to face the adversity lead their mouths to erupt and tell Moses, "listen dude! We were better off being slaves." They were basically saying, "we have given up our convenience of being in bondage just to follow you out here into a wilderness grave." They failed to understand that God made the promise through Moses.

When man makes the promise and fails, our conversation changes. This type of talk always proceeds out the mouth of someone who is not in agreement with you. You mean to tell me I let you into the chambers of my heart, you shared my bank account, we slept in the same bed, had intercourse, and now we're not getting married? I compromised my college degree, I put my business on hold, I refused a well-paying job offer to follow you into this wilderness you call a dream. This is why standing on what you believe before you agree is absolutely necessary. When there is no belief before agreement the unsettling dispute in your heart will keep arising.

Listen lady, if you're not in agreement then never be willing to compromise your legs being spread for a false promised land. Listen man, never be willing to compromise your leadership to indulge in any activity that delivers a mirage disguised as the promised land.

It's not like the Israelites did not have direction. God had given Moses clear direction on where they were going. It's not like the couple did not have direction either. God may have or may not have given them clear direction on where they should go. When the agreement is not solidified in the beginning, navigating through life becomes a frustration. The problem with man's GPS system is many of the functions are designed for our pleasure and not our purpose. God's GPS will always take you to your destination as long you stay committed and do not compromise the agreement. Now, in every relationship there will be times where we will have to compromise. It's a by-product of the mutual agreement you made. Knowing what you are not, will keep you from compromising who you are and keep you committed to the agreement you started with.

Just because we start out committed doesn't guarantee we will stay committed. Inside of the word commitment several words have been birthed. Words like responsibility, trust, loyalty and faithfulness. These words are key factors that act as cement in which the entire foundation sits on. Just because you have a solid foundation does not mean the house will not be disturbed. Remember in Matthew chapter 7 verse 25: [25]*Though the rain comes in torrents and the floodwaters rise and the winds beat against that house, it won't collapse because it is built on bedrock.*

In this verse it clearly tells you that your relationship will suffer, unless you have a strong foundation. The trials, winds and adversity will attempt to collapse what you built. After being together for eight years, in June, 2014 my wife and I faced a tsunami in our marriage. We had the rain, floodwaters and the winds smash against the house. This was one of the most devastating blows our relationship had ever experienced. During this process, while we contemplated divorce, we decided to separate, and thankfully the separation only lasted for four months.

During this period, I had an ample amount of time to sit by myself and survey the damage that had been done to our home. From my observation the structure had severe damage on all sides. The roof had been torn completely off. The walls were completely gone due to the floodwaters. The winds had tossed many of the items we held dear to our hearts and thought we could not live without. In the end, the frame of the house was still standing and the foundation was completely intact. I recall sitting in my mothers house going through the damage repeatedly in my mind.

I relived our awful arguments, the sounds of slamming doors, our silent dinners, the restless nights and the mutual agreement we had made. God began to remind me of the beginning stages of our marriage. We spent countless hours sitting with mature married couples who sat around having conversations about the Kingdom and the importance of building on a solid foundation. We made a mutual agreement to designate the majority of our time to sit at their feet and soak in as much information as possible. Little did we know a hurricane was headed right up on our marriage island years later. As ferocious as the storm may have been we survived to tell the story.

This situation strengthened my commitment and anchored my value system deep into the bedrock of my soul. I truly witnessed the Lord's hand holding our foundation together. For many of you, mutual agreement is a foreign language when it comes to trusting someone with your heart. Many of us have faced heartbreaks that seem irreparable. Many of you have given up hope in having anyone or even sacrificing your time again. The very thought of compromising again is so remote from your communication. I have come to reassure you that as long as you stick to the agreement and keep God at the center you can build again. First, my wife and I kept our agreement to God that we would keep Jesus at the center of our lives. Second, we would not compromise our foundation which was built on Him. Third, we would stay committed to each other in our journey. "Whatever you compromise to gain you will lose it every time".

Commitment is a rare characteristic in our current age. There are millions of things trying to grab our attention. We have social media and text messages constantly blasting notifications to our phones. We have become more committed to what we want versus what we need.

My business partner sat across a table from me in 2008 with plans of launching a beauty business that would impact the lives of people across the world. We sat at this table exchanging visions. Both of us were in the early phase of building something we believed would surpass us. I remember telling him about an outreach team I wanted to start and how it would spread across the entire globe. After pitching our visions back and forth we paused. He looked at me and said "what are you thinking?" At that very moment the value of our relationship was bubbling inside of me. I stared right in his eyes and said lets do it! Being cut from the streets, one thing I understood was loyalty, honor and especially commitment. Of course, with the streets came dishonor and broken loyalty as well.

At that moment I realized our verbal agreement was mutual. I was therefore committed to the journey despite whatever we would face. I was committed to building an outreach team that would spread across the globe in the face of adversity. I was committed to seeing his vision come to pass just as much as I was committed to seeing mine manifest. He was unaware a man named Anthony Wallace said something in November 2007 that stuck with me to this day. He said "If you submit your vision to another man's vision, it will come to pass."

Now when he said this, in my mind I didn't totally understand, but something in my spirit agreed instantly. Not too long after hearing that statement, it started to make sense in my heart and head. Of course do not submit your vision to just any person who comes along. I have learned that submission and commitment work very closely especially when forming a mutual agreement. When I sat across the table with my partner that day my heart was definitely in a submission position. I recognized that we both shared the same vision which was to transform peoples lives from a Kingdom's perspective through business. It didn't matter if he had the most amazing idea in the world. If we did not agree on the most important thing, which was the foundation, it would only be a matter of time before we crashed. I literally use this scripture as my relationship GPS. Amos chapter 3 verse 3: *Can two people walk together without agreeing on the direction?*

Since our meeting in 2008, he now has several beauty businesses named Oerigo Beauty in the United States and stretching far as the Middle East. I started the outreach team and it has become a global outreach team entitled C2BS (Cool2BSaved) in the United States and stretching far as the Middle East.

I am currently managing one of his beauty businesses in the state of Georgia. Periodically we speak and our language is still on the same page. We are still in agreement with the mission and committed to the vision. The funny part is that everything has only just begun. There have been a handful of times I had to compromise my time to support his vision and vice versa. Even as I sit writing this book, the value of our relationship has only increased because of the agreement we stand on. I now have several business relationships that I pour myself into. It's not because I'm looking for them to give me anything. It's because I have an understanding of the value of relationships. There is truly nothing they can give me that my Heavenly Father has not already given me. I also understand that whatever they do have, my Father is the provider of it all. This paradigm shift allowed me to discover when valuable people attract each other, their only desire is to exchange values so needs become nonexistent.

When you say you are committed to someone what does that actually mean? What does it look like? What does it feel like? I am constantly speaking with women and men of all ages telling me about how committed they are. I have spoken with young teens telling me about how committed they are. Subsequently, their idea of commitment has been perverted by the media or corrupted by unhealthy conversations.

Some people view commitment as two people who have been together for a substantial amount of time. However, it is possible to be connected with someone for a considerable amount of time and not be committed. Connection does not equal commitment. True commitment will always trace back to an agreement, and an agreement will always trace back to a foundation. Whenever we begin a relationship we should always keep the foundation, agreement, and commitment at the forefront of the conversation.

Recently someone asked me a question in reference to their relationship, "Do you think I should have to compete with his/her history or past relationships?" Before answering, I briefly meditated on the question for a few seconds. After assembling my thoughts I begin to direct this person back to the power of agreement. A person should never have to compete with anything in your past. I begin to explain the power of love. I do realize we live in a world where the word love is loosely used. When you love someone you will be able to see beyond their past and your focus will only be on the present. This depends on what you guys agreed to build on.

There are four different types of love I would like to explain. First, there is the love Eros where we get the word erotic. This love describes the sexual attraction someone may have for you. Second, there is phileo which extends the kind of love one would have towards a brother. This is where we get our word philadelphia, the city of brotherly love. Third, there is storge which extends the love one may have for a family member. The fourth is considered the agape love. This is considered the highest form of love. This love is the God-kind of love. Love is a powerful weapon if it is used in the correct manner.

If I build my relationship on Eros-love, what happens when the sexual flames are at an all time low? I may begin to think about you going back to your ex for the good-old times. Suppose you become injured in a terrible car accident and now you cannot perform in bed like you used to. The Eros foundation we built on begins to crash. Now we must remember this is what we both agreed to build on.

Now it may be one of the other two - phileo or storge. Either way, I have learned that the only way to look past a person's flaws is to have a mutual agreement that we are going to begin with Christ as the foundation, and keep Christ at the center as we build. Hence, we are not all going to agree on Christ being the center and circumference of the relationship. From personal experience I notice that when he is at the center I see my significant other differently. The culture is constantly attempting to convince you that there is no need for Jesus to sustain your relationship. There is no need to have him as the foundation. If he is at the center when I look at you I have to look through him to see you. Hence, when I look through him at you all I see is his quality traits not flaws. All I see is a mighty women not a nag, all I see is an outstanding man not a bum, all I see is God's daughter not a female dog, all I see is one of God's sons and not a sorry man.

Suppose he is not the center and the barber shop, nail salon, TV, gym, church or radio is the center. That means when I respond, I'll be speaking to you with whatever particular mediums are speaking. The enemy is not after your fancy title called marriage. He is not after the euphoria world you created during dating. He is after the power of the agreement. I'm going to show you exactly what he is after.

Matthew chapter 19 verses 4-5 states: *⁴"Haven't you read the Scriptures?" Jesus replied. "They record that from the beginning 'God made them male and female.' ⁵And he said, 'This explains why a man leaves his father and mother and is joined to his wife, and the two are united into one.'"*

I read over this passage numerous times until one day it became alive in my heart. I went from believing to receiving all that this passage meant. I thought to myself, it seems like they have more power being two rather than one. This is when God revealed to me, the power is not in the numbers, it's in the agreement. So the enemy, the media, the culture, is not after your marriage. They are after your agreement. Without the two becoming one, all you have is two people walking through life. There is no authentic agreement.

We can agree on certain things like a movie selection, restaurant, and even what vacations to take. Now when it comes to material objects or finances, we often run into a dilemma. The typical response is "don't forget that's my money", or "that's my car I had that before I met you". This is because the two never became one. This type of spirit is operating in the church today as well. Just because we're saved does not mean the two have become one. We can believe in Jesus but not receive all that he has to offer. Receiving him means I accept Matthew 19 verse 4-5. Becoming one changes your language from mine to ours, from your account to our account, from my car to our car, from my house to our house. This displays the value of a relationship at it's finest.

# SELF REFLECTION

# Chapter 3 The Benefits Of Going Deeper

There are numerous benefits that are connected with the value of a relationship. I'm learning on a continual basis the deeper I value, the more my life benefits. When we decide to invest ourselves, time, or money into people's lives the reciprocation is automatic. Luke painted a picture of this in Luke chapter 5 verses 1-7: *¹One day as Jesus was preaching on the shore of the Sea of Galilee, great crowds pressed in on him to listen to the word of God. ²He noticed two empty boats at the water's edge, for the fishermen had left them and were washing their nets. ³Stepping into one of the boats, Jesus asked Simon, its owner, to push it out into the water. So he sat in the boat and taught the crowds from there. ⁴When he had finished speaking, he said to Simon, "Now go out where it is deeper, and let down your nets to catch some fish." ⁵"Master," Simon replied, "we worked hard all last night and didn't catch a thing. But if you say so, I'll let the nets down again." ⁶And this time their nets were so full of fish they began to tear! ⁷A shout for help brought their partners in the other boat, and soon both boats were filled with fish and on the verge of sinking.*

This passage shifted my entire paradigm of how I viewed my relationship with mankind. It allowed me to tap into another value that I never had before. The people were pressed in on Jesus listening to him teach. As they were close to him, he noticed two empty boats at the water's edge. Now Simon and the crew had been fishing all night. They were in their father's fishing business and were very skilled at their profession. They went from fishing all day to being on the edge of the shore washing their nets. They were finished with the business for the day, they were finished dealing with the kids, they were finished dealing with the marriage, and they were finished dealing with the boss.

Then here comes this guy name Jesus stepping into one of the boats requesting that Simon push it out into the water. I could imagine Simon thinking, "We have been out here fishing all day and you want me to push the boat back out into the water." Then he goes on to tell Simon "Now go out where it is deeper, and let down your nets to catch some fish." This conversation between Jesus and Simon is very intriguing. Jesus finds Simon in a phase of giving up and he's pushing him to go deeper. Jesus was pressed by a crowd and managed to notice two empty boats.

Have you ever been pressed by circumstances, obstacles, family concerns, personal business and had the ability to look out of your turmoil into another persons situation? He locates Simon in his fishing business and encourages him to go out a little deeper. If the people within your circle are not challenging you to go deeper then it may be time to reevaluate your circle.

These men had been fishing for years and their world was just interrupted by this stranger walking along the shore. Jesus is being bombarded by crowds of people wanting to hear more about His Kingdom. Instead he ceases speaking and detects a needy situation. Putting yourself in someone else's dilemma requires true selflessness. Jesus didn't see a burden, he saw a benefit. Going deeper gives you insight to look pass the current issue. Instead of a problem, you see opportunity. The opportunity has benefits connected to it that can only be discovered when going deeper. Simon and the crew had been fishing and did not catch anything.

Imagine working on the relationship, giving it all you have and there is no transformation taking place. You are working at a job with a manager who continues to test your patience daily. You are dealing with a marriage where forgiveness has become a foreigner and you have said sorry for the last time. When giving up feels like the best option and someone says "I need you to go a little deeper".

After looking into Simon's hopelessness, Jesus tells Simon "I want you to throw your net out again so you can catch some fish". I'm going to need you to forgive him or her one more time. I'm going to need you to talk to your son one more time. Please have patience with your daughter just one more time. I know the job seems hopeless but hang in there just one more day.

By this point Simon begins to read Jesus his resume. Listen Jesus, I don't think you heard me the first time. We have been working all night and we didn't catch a thing. I have been dealing with this women for 13 years she will never understand. I have been dealing with this man for six months he is just an idiot like his dad, and is stubborn to the bone. I have been dealing with these kids since birth and it's going to take a miracle for them to listen. This girl treats me like trash and has the nerve to walk in my house pregnant. To make matters worse, her brother is locked up downtown and keeps calling me for bail money. I refuse to deal with my manager any longer. I have been in this same position before and I don't see any hopes of increase. I'm disgusted with my family telling me how much of a disappoint I am to them.

These are usually the replies you receive whenever you challenge someone to go a little deeper. Simon lays out his brief resume and then responds to Jesus. Since you requested me to go out a little deeper, I will. Now in Luke chapter 5 verse 6: *⁶And this time their nets were so full of fish they began to tear!* And this time the marriage papers were picked up off the table and torn up. And this time forgiveness broke through the hurt and betrayal and love prevailed. And this time the kids were reconciled with the parents. And this time the young lady was united with her mother having an intimate conversation about her future grand baby. And this time the promotion came, and this time the managers perspective of the employee was altered, and this time, and this time, and this time! I need to you think about your dilemma, your mess, your circumstance and say "This time it will be different!"

The verses clearly state that when Simon chose to go a little deeper, their nets were so full of fish they began to tear. There was no room for Simon to react on his emotions. I could imagine him feeling like not going a little deeper. I could imagine a lot of us not feeling like going a little deeper. Especially when the relationship you are in has not been favorable to you.

I believe we cross paths with people every day who challenge us to go a little deeper in a particular area of our lives. Jesus arrives on the scene and completely interrupted the way Simon and the crew were accustomed to doing business. Their entire world was rearranged from a simple act of obedience. Jesus understood the value of relationships and had insight to see how one event was connected to the next. The true value was not in their fishing business. The true value was locked inside of Simon and it took him going deeper to unlock his full potential. The story continues in Luke chapter 5 verse 7: *⁷A shout for help brought their partners in the other boat, and soon both boats were filled with fish and on the verge of sinking.*

When you chose to go deeper in your relationship did it cause you to shout for help and tell somebody? The fishing business was mediocre until they went out a little deeper. Now they had to call in reinforcement. Your business may be doing okay until you chose to go a little deeper. Now you need to call for partners. The verse states they had so much fish they were on the verge of sinking. God did not need Simon's fishing business to make him rich. Not to say, the value of your business will not make you prosperous. At the end of the day the benefits of going deeper were connected to something more substantial. As you continue to read the story in Luke chapter 5 verses 8-11, it reveals why Jesus looked beyond the crowd pressing in on him: *⁸When Simon Peter realized what had happened, he fell to his knees before Jesus and said, "Oh, Lord, please* leave me-I'm such a sinful man." [9]For he was awestruck by the number of fish they had caught, as were the others with him. [10]His partners, James and John, the sons of Zebedee, were also amazed. Jesus replied to Simon, "Don't be afraid! From now on you'll be fishing for people!" [11]And as soon as they landed, they left everything and followed Jesus.

The Bible states in Luke chapter 5 verse 8, Simon realized what happened and fell to his knees. It's in this moment Simon discovers how much he needed grace to go deeper. He was in awe of what just occurred with his business.

Even the people connected to him were astonished. In this instant Jesus replies "Don't worry about what you were incapable of doing, don't be sad about the problem you couldn't overcome". Simon is about to receive his mission and benefit package like you and I when we choose to go deeper. Jesus replies "Simon saying from now on you'll be fishing for people". Luke chapter 5 verse 11 goes on to say as soon as they landed, they left everything and followed Jesus.

If we pay close attention to the story, Simon assumed his true value was in the fishing business. Imagine if Simon would have been attached to the miracle that just occurred with his business. How often do we become attached to the problem or miracle instead of the opportunity they present? Simon received the miracle, fell to his knees and recognized he was unworthy of receiving such a blessing. He had just experienced favor in his business. From the initiation of Jesus spotting the two empty boats, His end game was to transform Simon from a fishing man into someone who fished for people. In between the miracle and Simon going to fish for people was an act of surrender. I believe Jesus did not want Simon touching the people without recognizing he himself needed just as much grace and love.

The people in your business, your marriage, your family, your ministry whom you are going to touch are considered high value in the Kingdom of God. Trust, the benefits of going deeper is not connected to your pockets it's connected to the people. Everyone loves benefits especially when it benefits you. Benefits are defined as an advantage or profit gained from something. There are various types of benefits that exist. People receive benefit packages from their job such as medical, life, disability and 401k's, etc. The Kingdom of Heaven also offers a benefit package. This package is received upon us believing and accepting Jesus into our lives. We begin to experience a lot more of these benefits when we go deeper into our relationship. Now I'm not speaking of the word "deep" in terms of intellectual or theological depth. I'm referring to the depth of relationship. I have discovered this depth in the value of relationship. Even when I have been devalued, I have discovered my job is to value others.

It was not comfortable for me when people would devalue me. I can tell you now, it took me discovering who I was that allowed me to respond in love. Nobody wants to be devalued when you're constantly pouring out love and only receiving hate. You need to understand there will be moments where there is nobody there to encourage you. In these moments everything you learned or said you believed in will be tested. In these moments your parents are unavailable, your mentors are out of town on a meeting and his/her phone is out of service. The pastor is not accepting any calls or emails while he/she is on vacation. Your wife, husband, boyfriend, girlfriend and even the kids are completely out of answers. This can be a very lonesome place from which to transition. The feeling of being abandoned and unwanted can create a mindset that wants to give up. You went from being encouraged about your empty situation, to being provoked to go out into the deep, to going out and touching the people, to nobody around to talk with.

Silence is a perfect place for God's voice to be fine-tuned in your life. There will come a Gethsemane in all of our lives. The garden of Gethsemane is an interesting place, located at the foot of the Mount of Olives in Jerusalem, and is most famous as the place where Jesus prayed and his disciples slept the night before Jesus' crucifixion.

In Matthew chapter 26 versus 36-44, *36Then Jesus went with them to the olive grove called Gethsemane, and he said, "Sit here while I go over there to pray." 37He took Peter and Zebedee's two sons, James and John, and he became anguished and distressed. 38He told them, "My soul is crushed with grief to the point of death. Stay here and keep watch with me." 39He went on a little farther and bowed with his face to the ground, praying, "My Father! If it is possible, let this cup of suffering be taken away from me. Yet I want your will to be done, not mine." 40Then he returned to the disciples and found them asleep. He said to Peter, "Couldn't you watch with me even one hour? 41Keep watch and pray, so that you will not give in to temptation. For the spirit is willing, but the body is weak!" 42Then Jesus left them a second time and prayed, "My Father! If this cup cannot be taken away unless I drink it, your will be done." 43When he returned to them again, he found them sleeping, for they couldn't keep their eyes open. 44So he went to pray a third time, saying the same things again.*

It's in this garden scene that the value of relationship is challenged by Jesus' disciples and strengthened by His Father. Your Gethsemane is always a place of solitude where it's just you and the Creator. Nothing about this scene depicts joy, happiness, winning or even victory. This is the moment where Jesus is about to be betrayed and crucified. Pay close attention because in the benefits of going deeper you are going to suffer and something you hold dear will have to die. It may be a boyfriend that you believe is your king sent from heaven. It may be the girlfriend who captivated your heart and you cannot see yourself with nobody else. It may be the job you have been holding on to for the last few years because it gives you a sense of value and security but you dread everyday walking into the building. It may be the crew that is asking you to sacrifice your time every weekend to go out and party.

The benefits of going deeper does not always look appealing but the fruit does. Jesus is about to be crucified. He's asking his disciples to watch and pray so you do not fall into temptation. He is praying in agony with distress covering his countenance. His voice cries out "*Father please let this cup pass me*". I know if Jesus was at that point of caving in, we are not far from it. I have felt like giving up numerous times. I had nobody to call and wanted the pain to leave. When you are going deeper and you are isolated everything in you is saying "I'm done". Not only are you in anguish, your friends are sleeping while you suffer. Jesus returns to his disciples after praying only to find them sleeping. Don't be discouraged, when you see your lifelines sleeping when you need them the most. The benefits of going deeper takes you from your will to thy will. Jesus makes a comment in his prayer "*Yet I want your will to be done, not mine*". The entire scene prior to his crucification was not even about him. Your suffering, your agony, your pain, your triumph, your victory, your crushed soul is not even about you. Imagine if Jesus would have given up and relinquished his authority over flesh. Instead, he saw down the corridors of time and he noticed you, he noticed me, and his resilience allowed him to go deeper. He valued us so much he gave his life. The benefits of going deeper is not connected to your pockets it's connected to the people. There are family members whose success rate is contingent upon you deciding to go a little more deeper.

# SELF REFLECTION

# Chapter 4 Maintaining Through It All

It is very critical that while building relationships we do not force ourselves into peoples lives. Forced relationships usually take a drastic turn and become more of manipulation verses relation. I recall a time in my life attempting to put two family members back together. I kept trying to get them to communicate but found myself frustrated after several attempts and no cooperation from either party. I soon discovered forced growth always leads to manipulation. It was in my frustration I saw the image of a screw. Since I was a kid God would show me images and follow with a word, then a sentence and then an entire story. From the depiction of the screw I realized why the relationship was not working. I was putting a demand on this relationship to work utilizing the wrong tools.

If any of you have ever put anything together like a bike, piece of furniture, toy or electronics, suppose you have a 1/2 inch screw and you are attempting to place it inside of a 1/4 inch hole. Through simple math and observation you can clearly see the 1/2 inch screw is not going to fit in a hole that small. So you purchase the tricycle and while putting it together you force the 1/2 inch screw into the 1/4 inch hole. Now, we know it doesn't fit so we manipulate the screw to make it work.

Perhaps the sofa doesn't fit through the door, so we use a bit of manipulation to squeeze it through the door. Hopefully we don't scratch the leather or damage the framing. A lot of energy was put behind forcefully positioning the screw into the hole. We now have a well assembled mess. Since the screw was forced in, when it is time to operate the bike the dysfunctional characteristics are obvious to everyone. The bike doesn't ride straight, there is a squeaking noise on the right wheel where the screw was manipulated. The family members were still disputing. My mediation was failing at every attempt. The more I manipulated, the more furious everyone became. Once the screw is forced in, there is even more of a complication when trying to pull it out. Since you had to use manipulation to get the screw in you will need to use manipulation to get the screw out. In the process of getting the screw out it's a strong possibility you will strip the threads off the screw.

Way too often we force ourselves into relationships by manipulation. Even when it doesn't work we are determined to make it work. There's always a since of gratification once we're in. It's in the exit where we experience the threads stripping away. We lose our identity while going in and coming out. Many relationships have lost their threads through manipulation and forced entry. My objective in this chapter is to give you some illustrations on how to maintain through it all. How do we maintain the value through manipulation, through being hurt and dealing with unforgiving circumstances?

I find it astonishing that when you and I were created we had something placed in us called homeostasis. Homeostasis is two words combined. *Homeo* meaning the same, and *stasis* meaning staying. This term refers to the body's ability to maintain a stable internal environment in response to a changing external environment. When your body achieves homeostasis, the conditions in your body remain the same despite the many changes outside.

For example, in a healthy person their body temperature stays at 98.6 degrees Fahrenheit even when the room temperature increases to 100 degrees. Now there are times when the mechanisms that control this do not work properly due to poor habits. When this occurs we have what is called homeostatic imbalance which is associated with various disorders. Staying the same can be wearisome when trying to maintain the value of relationship that seems unmanageable and the person or persons are uncooperative. Not only do we have to manage our personal lives. We have to navigate through this imperfect world. A world that is constantly trying to convince you to sacrifice your God given stability in exchange for it's culture of frailty.

I believe as humans we intuitively search for a utopian world. We have a burning desire for our relationships to be continually wrapped in euphoria. This delight is shared in countless relationships across the globe. The question still remains, how do we sustain the relationship when the value system has been compromised, diminished or is nonexistent?

The young boy or girl who grows up in a poverty-stricken neighborhood filled with crime, drugs, death, and disease has an unconventional view of what's valuable. To this young person, the value of a meal is more important than going to school. Their choices are limited and crime may be the only option to acquire a daily meal. The value of selling drugs and committing a crime is more important, especially since nobody has told them otherwise. Their entire environment permeates with the stench of destruction.

Some young ladies have never been told they are valuable unless sexual intercourse was involved in the equation. Some young boys have never been told they are unique and have the ability to do anything they put their minds to. For many of the young lives that share these conditions, they were birthed into turmoil by parents who suffer from their own identity crisis. This is why it's essential we inject the value of relationship back into the family structure. Our moral leaders have been replaced with money chasers and charlatans. Wrong is right and right is wrong. Generational curses have suffocated the air out of our righteous behavior. God needs to be forged back in the center of the family unit. Pride needs to be replaced with humility. Our kids need to learn that forgiveness does not mean you're feeble or less of a human. This is an internal process that is not developed overnight. When we reach the level of knowing who we are internally, our resistance to the environment surrounding us becomes less threatening. Remember, homeostasis refers to the body's ability to maintain a stable internal environment in response to a changing external environment. In most cases forgiveness is required to break free from the mental and physical imprisonment.

Forgiveness is one of the most powerful ingredients when it comes to establishing a fortified relationship. It's an expression of how much you value the person beyond what he or she has done to you. It clears away certain attributes that accompany manipulation and being hurt. These attributes include such feelings as bitterness, anger, resentment, revenge, frustration and especially hate. If we are not careful our hurt can easily turn into hate. Occasionally the threads in the relationship have been stripped and the situation seems irreparable. Whether we believe it or not, forgiveness has the power to destroy these attributes that squeeze the love out of relationships. These attributes may seem harmless, but anyone of them can cause serious damage if left unresolved.

These are the same attributes that destroy the value of nations around the world. The young man may still be holding onto the fact that his mother gave him up for adoption, although she provided reasons for her decisions and pleaded for forgiveness. He is still unwilling to forgive her after having to live with the repercussions of her decisions. The husband whose wife committed adultery lives in constant fear of being hurt again. His heart has become numb to loving anyone, in hopes that he can avoid the painful experience of betrayal entering his life again.

In these examples internal stability has been shattered. Forgiving someone seems belittling to the person offering the forgiveness, especially if they have proof of not being at fault. It's not a matter of fault when true forgiveness is being offered. The question remains, what if they never apologize to me? The answer is, true forgiveness doesn't look for an apology.

# SELF REFLECTION

# Chapter 5 The Lease Agreement

Not too long ago I was thinking about renting a home. After researching a few places I located a place for rent at a reasonable price. I remember calling the number on the ad and spoke with the gentlemen who had his contact information listed as the owner of the property. We set up a meeting where I could go and view the property. When I went to view the property the layout was exactly how it was displayed on the website. The images did no justice to actually standing inside of the home. Immediately I called the gentlemen back and I wanted to discuss how I could obtain this home. He began to tell me how this particular property was being viewed by several applicants and was not going to be on the market long. He then began to tell me that if I wanted to secure this property I needed to send him the security deposit and he would pull it off the market. I informed him that I would be willing to send him the deposit as soon as I received a copy of the lease agreement to review the terms and conditions. He was not willing to send me a copy of the lease prior to me sending any of the funds he requested, therefore we did not move forward with process. Later on after doing some research I discovered the gentlemen was a fraud acting as the owner of the property. The entire deal was a scam from the beginning.

This incident immediately had me take at deeper look at the value of relationships from a lease perspective. Investopedia defines leases as "A legal and binding contracts that set forth the terms of rental agreements in real estate". If you decide you want to rent a property, there will be a lease prepared by the property manager or landlord. In the lease it will have information such as terms, security deposit, duration of lease, whether or not you can have pets on the premises, and how many occupants will be dwelling in the apartment. When the lease is signed both parties agree to the terms prior to the tenant occupying the place.

I've had countless conversations where men and women have deposited their money, time, heart and mind and have not even looked over the lease. We need to remember we don't own anyone. The dog is not yours, and the kids are not yours. The wife, husband, boyfriend, or girlfriend are not yours. They are all on loan until their duration on Earth expires. We don't take time to look at what's outlined in this relationship. We tend to believe that he or she promising to discuss the terms later will suffice. Imagine if I would have given that guy my money without viewing the actual lease. He would have taken my money and disappeared. I would have been depositing my money monthly into a fraudulent account.

Getting into a relationship without knowing the terms can lead to extreme consequences. He may have the mindset of month-to-month while she is thinking long-term. He may be thinking of a picket fence with a dog and two kids, and she is thinking one child and no dog. In my previous chapter on mutual agreement, words like contract, covenant and binding are very familiar terms. This is very essential information that should be discussed during the early stages of the dating process so you will know exactly what you are about to deposit your time, mind, money, heart and effort into. I would dare to say we need to discuss our terms during the first date. You may need to receive the lease right away depending how interested you are. At least this gives you an ample amount of time to go home and review what you're stepping into before you construct any further obligations.

I believe we can spend a day with someone and make a conscious decision if we are going to allot them another day. Then after a week, you can determine if you will allot them another week. Time is extremely valuable and way too often we bind ourselves by walking into relationships blinded by the external features.

I love the way the dictionary defines deposit. Used as a verb, it means to store or entrust with someone for safekeeping. What have you stored or entrusted someone with for safe keeping? How many installments have you made before reading the fine print? How much have you unloaded of yourself into them? These are serious questions we need to ask ourselves. Typically the ecstasy has us fascinated to the extent we fail to notice pertinent details about the individual we're entertaining.

Mr. and Mrs. Edwards had been looking at a few properties for several months. Their real estate agent has even sent them some potential listings which fit the description of what they desired. This was a huge move for them both, so they intended on leasing a townhouse for a year before purchasing a home in the area. Getting a sense of the neighborhood and what it has to offer was one of their major concerns. They were also keeping in perspective things such as crime, a local park for Mr. Edwards to walk his dogs, proximity of shopping centers and the travel distance of Mrs. Edwards' job, are significant factors. After sitting down with a trusted agent and reviewing the terms with the lease agreement they decided to sign an one-year contract. Taking all of this into consideration, why would we approach relationships any differently?

Now in no way am I saying that he or she is a piece of property, although in actuality they all are. I believe we are all God's property. Perhaps when you met him or her you may not have looked at the relationship as a lease agreement pertaining to a piece of property. However, we are constantly entrusting individuals with things we hold valuable to us, and then proceeding without asking any prudent questions.

Let's make this clear, nobody wants to be under a sublease so please ask questions. He or she may be into having multiple partners. I know it sounds absurd, but welcome to our new generation. If your desire is to be married you may want to ask him or her if they have the same desire. If so, then when? If your desire is to have kids you may want to share that during the romantic candlelight dinner. If he or she doesn't, then you know how to proceed before depositing any more time. Not having kids may be something within the lease you're not willing to compromise.

Maybe he wants to practice celibacy until marriage. You may decide that after a few months he will change his mind. Or, maybe he's not willing to compromise to these terms. Hopefully this is discussed during the candlelight dinner or during a long walk through the park with the fall leaves dropping around these potential lesses. One party may say "I understand what you're taking about. Give me about two months, six more months, a year and I promise we are going to get married". The question you should ask yourself is, "How can somebody promise you something if they can't guarantee it"? They are not even promising you tomorrow, let alone the day or time they said it in.

# SELF REFLECTION

# Chapter 6 Business And Pleasure

One of the greatest downfalls as a business owner is attempting to run a business without a plan. If there is no plan, your business is subject to whatever life brings. As a business owner, we make decisions that will effect not only us, but numerous people that are connected to us. Millions of business owners across the world have strengths and weaknesses that will propel them into a greater success or disable the company completely.

One person may be highly effective in brand building and business planning, but when pleasure is blended into the equation, the structure they designed runs the risk of becoming imbalanced. This is a common area I have familiarized myself with over the years as an entrepreneur, and as someone who has assisted with the building of several successful companies. Realistically, I believe you can blend the two worlds together if your value system is in order. You may have to modify what you consider to be business and what you consider to be pleasure. What you consider pleasure may be pleasant, but is it profitable to your business in the long term? Every pleasure comes with consequences whether it's healthy or unhealthy. As entrepreneurs, we enjoy having the freedom that business ownership creates. It also creates a loneliness that is often not communicated verbally so many business owners conceal their pain behind what they consider to be pleasure.

Let me reiterate that pleasure does not make you a careless person. I believe as business-minded individuals we need to readjust our lens to how we view mixing these two areas together. I have met a number of couples who have mixed business with pleasure and are living a well-balanced life. A large majority of these couples are happily married. Someone may ask, "do you believe you can date someone and still be their business partner"? My reply would be "Of course you can".

It's not until we bring sexual intercourse into the equation that our perception gets distorted. Sex has a tendency of spinning a business partnership into a whirlwind. The majority of business owners are constantly on the move, trying to advance to the next level, improving the quality of their company, increasing sales, managing their personal life and also thinking of the next great idea. The question remains, how do I find time to squeeze a relationship into my chaotic schedule? This question is not a matter of finding time as much as it is in making time. We make time for what is important. If having a valuable relationship is important then we will make time. A busy schedule should never be the answer for slowing down to indulge in brief intimacy.

Brief intimacy always starts off as an innocent motive with no strings attached. Emotions are a pair of strings that cannot stay detached when intimacy continues to occur. When we have no intentions of building a longevity with him or her. The very strings we swore were not attached, will turn into the ropes that begin to link, fasten or connect our souls for the right or wrong reasons. Hopefully we connect for the reason of having a long-term agreement versus an one-night stand. Remember when you said you didn't have time for a relationship? It's amazing what lonely people find time for.

The process of designing, launching and running a new business is definitely time-consuming. As a business owner, it's filled with long hours and plenty of risks. Our minds are constantly consumed with innovative thoughts associated with managing our business. Regardless of your accolades and economic status, nobody is immune to the temptation of mixing business and pleasure. Mixing the two can lead to trust issues and potentially a loss in productivity. Not only do relationships between employer and employee lead to a lack of influence, it can lead to complications which affect the company's character.

As stated in the first chapter of building blocks, the beginning stages are so vital. There are different types of pleasure in every relationship. Your pleasure may be surfing the Internet viewing social media during company hours. Your pleasure may be drinking alcohol with the new assistant after work. Either way you are still mixing business with pleasure. Every business owner's mind may not be to engage in a romantic endeavor. I do believe people can conduct a healthy relationship and keep it strictly-business. I believe we need to be mindful of how we define business in order to avoid jeopardizing our character for a network connection.

One of the best ways to develop a business with potential clients is to establish boundaries for yourself that you will not compromise. As I mentioned in the lease agreement, make sure your terms are clear about what you stand for and what you will not tolerate. A lot of entrepreneurs I speak with suffer from what I like to call "creative disaster". They have some of the most innovative minds I have encountered. Some have the intentions of working for attention. Innovative minds that crave attention usually search for opportunities to mix business and pleasure. When you crave attention eventually that craving can turn into a burning desire to covet anything that will satisfy your appetite. For one business owner it may be drugs, for one it may be sex, for one it may be more money and for another it may be food. Everybody's desert is different and how you quench your thirst while in that desert, is contingent upon your choice of pleasure. This is not a message of condemnation toward anyone who is engaging in any of the scenarios depicted. I'm simply stressing the fact that in order to run a successful business we need to exhibit guidelines that we are not willing to compromise, while understanding that each pleasure comes with a risk that can ultimately effect the rewards.

I have discovered that best way to blend the two is to continually assess and review the structure of your foundation. This will require work and an architectural mindset. Trust, I believe you can do it and will do it. The very fact that you are reading this book lets me know that you want to. With that being said, I leave you with some of my key ingredients that have helped me survive through the temptations.

The 3Gs that men or women fall victim to:

For guys it will be:
   Gold - money
   Glitter - materials
   Girls - sex

For women it will be:
   Gold - money
   Glitter - materials
   Guys - sex

1 Corinthians 3 verses 10-12 *[10]Because of God's grace to me, I have laid the foundation like an expert builder. Now others are building on it. But whoever is building on this foundation must be very careful. [11]For no one can lay any foundation other than the one we already have-Jesus Christ.*

*[12]Anyone who builds on that foundation may use a variety of materials; gold, silver, jewels, wood, hay, or straw. [13]But there will come a time, fire will reveal what kind of work each builder has done. The fire will show if a person's work has any value.*

# SELF REFLECTION

# Chapter 7 The Sheep, The Coin, The Son
## Found in Luke 15:1:32

Nothing has impacted my life more than these three parables written in the Bible. Concealed in these three stories, Jesus expresses his deep concern about the lost and the found. I believe the value of a relationship places a tremendous amount of emphasis on people who may have been displaced or abandoned. The very fact of losing someone or something that is dear to our hearts can be devastating.

Think about it, why would a man leave his ninety-nine sheep to go and find the one he lost? Why would a women with ten coins sweep through her entire house searching for the one coin she lost? Why would a father whose son ran off and totally disrespected him by squandering his inheritance celebrate his son's return?

The amount of loss never mattered in these three scenarios. In order to understand the value of these parables we need to place ourselves inside the story. I constantly make a conscious effort to evaluate every relationship that enters and exits my life. Carefully assessing them allows me to gain access into the true value of what it is I possess. I realize I am to be a steward over these relationships whether it be monetary, objects, or people. All of us have been like sheep and wandered off away from our purpose. I don't believe people intentionally want to be lost. We all have been misplaced like the coin needing to be sought after. The prodigal son dealt with his rejection by taking his inheritance and withdrawing from the family. Whether it be deliberately or accidental, there is always hope of restoring what has been lost.

Isaiah chapter 53 verse 6 *"All of us, like sheep, have strayed away."*

Before we continue, let's get a clear understanding of the definition of a parable. A parable is a short story that teaches a moral or spiritual lesson. I could imagine the shepherd frantically searching for the one sheep that wandered away. If a sheep wandered off, it was left vulnerable to the wolves that roamed around. Now the shepherd's job was to tend to the sheep. The shepherd was responsible for feeding and guarding the sheep in the valleys throughout the region.

History speaks of sheep being integrated into people's family along with other animals such as a chicken or a pig. This integration revealed the value that was connected to these animals, especially the sheep. In Luke chapter 5 verse 5 it says *"And when he has found it, he will joyfully carry it home on his shoulders"*. There will be relationships in your life where people you value and consider family may need you to carry them home on your shoulders. Perhaps they were in the wilderness in a position of disfavor, surrounded by a damaged environment and no longer with the flock. Maybe they lost sight of the ones who truly loved them. The sheep usually wandered off away from the flock or the family. Nothing creates a sense of loneliness like being isolated in the wilderness without someone to cover you. You go from being covered to being vulnerable to the unfamiliar territory that has wrapped around you. In the midst of a deserted landscape the shepherd, the wife, the husband, or the friend leaves what needs their immediate attention to seek after you. It says the shepherd had one hundred sheep and one wandered off. So he left the ninety-nine in the wilderness to go find that one. The value placed on that one sheep was immaculate.

The parable of the coin places a deep emphasis on being complete versus incomplete. In Luke chapter 15 *"Or suppose a woman has ten silver coins and loses one. Won't she light a lamp and sweep the entire house and search carefully until she finds it?"*

I don't believe anyone likes to feel devalued or neglected. I have a methodology I created titled GTSA which means *"gathered together, scattered apart"*. In relationships you can sometimes feel like you are scattered. I believe it relates to the woman having a set of coins that were together and now she is searching the entire house to find the missing piece. Her mind is in a scattered state. Whenever people are scattered they usually feel incomplete and unnoticed. Here this lady is with an incomplete coin set. The relationship of her set is meaningless without the missing coin. The value was placed on the coin being a complete set.

Whenever people are together in their mind, at home, or with their finances there is a sense of completion. I don't know about you, but I prefer to have my life gathered together versus scattered apart. Suppose you walk into someone's home and the kid's toys are tossed all over the floor. The dog is over in the corner using the bathroom. You walk into the kitchen to get some water and there are dirty dishes piled up in the sink. From this picture I would say things are scattered.

I have learned that being scattered effects your ability to think clearly. Not knowing where something is can effect the way you communicate. Being scattered creates an atmosphere of discomfort. Nothing kills creativity like being scattered. A scattered environment produces an uncomfortable darkness that blinds you from the truth. In a gathered environment people are susceptible to open up and to relax. They feel like they are not being overlooked by the clutter of life. Your mind is more at peace when you know where things are. Nothing helps relieve scattered thoughts like a light being lit, in the midst of a dark world with so many scattered relationships. There needs to be a light shed upon every area ranging from financial, marital, parental, education, entrepreneurship, friendship, and many other aspects of a relationship. This is the only way we can find what is missing and return back to the foundation to have a complete set. Remember the Bible said the lady lit a lamp and swept through the entire room carefully searching for the coin. This suggests that we must be intentionally attentive to the relationships around us. You may be the very answer to someone being complete.

Each parable has taught me a valuable lesson in reference to not throwing people away. I have found the importance of not being judgmental when people go astray by studying the sheep. The value in the coin story allowed me to see how our lives are not always complete. It's in the scattered moments that we realize what's important in our lives. Out of all of the stories no parable has touched my heart more than the parable of the prodigal son. Maybe you could not relate to the sheep. Perhaps you have no money issues and your life is complete. This parable of the prodigal son displays a level of love that reflects the heart of God toward us in so many ways. I have literally learned so much about myself and others through living this parable. I have become more knowledgeable about the power of forgiveness. The father has two sons and the younger son basically says I want my half of the money before you die. To make matters worse, a few days later he packs his bags, moves to a distant town and after a while all of his money ran out. There was a drought in the city and food became scarce. He went from being in an adequate estate to an inadequate waste land.

Imagine being in a relationship with someone you spent years with, or having a child you raised decide they are taking their share of what you built and leaving immediately. The feeling of being rejected can cause hatred to settle in our hearts in both cases. This is where another level of forgiveness needs to be extended. What do you do when someone you have invested your heart, mind, time and money into decides you're no longer of any value to them?

There are many questions that will attempt to bombard your mind. How could they just leave me like that? I wonder if they ever cared for me? Are they okay? What if we never speak again? These questions can be overwhelming if they are not handled correctly. I believe the father in this story paints a great example of how to care for someone who has not only been rejected, but the recipient as well. In the story it states while the son was returning home his father was filled with love and compassion. He ran to his son, embraced him, and kissed him. He then begins to tell his servants to prepare a meal as we are going to celebrate my son's return. He was once lost, but now he is found. He was once dead, but now he is alive. When you examine the story you will find that the older brother was not so enthusiastic about his younger brother's return. After carefully reading this parable there are three points that were noticeable to me.

Three points to gather insight from: Luke chapter 15 verses 12-13 *¹²The younger son told his father, 'I want my share of your estate now before you die.' So his father agreed to divide his wealth between his sons. ¹³"A few days later this younger son packed all his belongings and moved to a distant land, and there he wasted all his money in wild living.*

## 1. Enter or Leaving Prematurely

The scripture above allowed me to see how in relationships we either enter or leave prematurely. Sometimes we are not prepared for the relationship but we disregard the signs and make a grand entrance. Way too often we want what we want and so we get what we get. The situation may not be going how we expect so we make an exit to avoid the process. Process is a necessity that many of us try so hard to avoid. By avoiding the process we may begin to lose the very relationships we wanted so desperately. The young son left prematurely. He insisted on having his share of the estate before his father died.

Luke chapter 15 verse 16-17 *¹⁶The young man became so hungry that even the pods he was feeding the pigs looked good to him. ¹⁷But no one gave him anything. "When he finally came to his senses, he said to himself, 'At home even the hired servants have food enough to spare, and here I am dying of hunger!'"*

## 2. Hunger Distorted His Vision

The young man went from leaving his father's home with his wealth and starting his journey in life. He cuts the relationship between the one who was feeding him and finds himself eating with pigs. The wrong appetite can often lead to a path we didn't desire. It can distort our vision to the point that what's unhealthy for us seems like a meal fit for a King or Queen. After receiving no help he came to his senses. Nothing brings us to our senses like life striking you to the ground.

Luke chapter 15 verses 28-32 "[28]*The older brother was angry and wouldn't go in. His father came out and begged him.* [29]*But he replied, 'All these years I've slaved for you and never once refused to do a single thing you told me to. And in all that time you never gave me even one young goat for a feast with my friends.* [30]*Yet when this son of yours comes back after squandering your money on prostitutes, you celebrate by killing the fattened calf!'* [31]*"His father said to him, 'Look, dear son, you have always stayed by me, and everything I have is yours.* [32]*We had to celebrate this happy day. For your brother was dead and has come back to life! He was lost, but now he is found!'"*

### 3. Life After Death

Maybe you found yourself starting and leaving prematurely. Perhaps you thought the person or business you signed up for was going to change your life forever. Your hunger for the now and not the process convinced you it would be easy to leave and live how you felt. I'm sure that relationship forced you to mature quickly. The divorce you are going through or you have experienced feels like death while you're breathing. The closest ones to you may have written you off as dead and gone. I'm so glad the father decided to rejoice and celebrate with his son who was once dead and now back to life. Along this journey through life we must remember that we are dying daily and not everyone is going to celebrate you coming back to life.

# SELF REFLECTION

# Chapter 8 The Power Of Forgiveness

Nothing attacks the heart like unpleasant times. We all have experienced some form of suffering whether it was intentional or unintentional. This type of pain creates a discomfort that can cause emotional, mental, physical and spiritual damage. Perhaps the pain was caused by a relative, a co-worker, a friend, a spouse, a parent, your kids, society, the government or maybe the pain was even self-inflicted. Either way, how we react to the damage is crucial to our recovery.

I have witnessed so many people who have taken devastating blows, and allowed their hurt to lead them to a life of isolation or rebellion. I have been the recipient and deliverer of unforgiving packages more than once. Of course the wrong-doing is much easier to digest when it's not being directed toward you. However, when the darts are being targeted at your heart, the guilt and shame it releases are like bacteria left in an open wound. Many of us have been wounded by circumstances in life and not taken or given ourselves the appropriate time to heal. Without taking the proper time to heal we can find ourselves bleeding over everyone we come in contact with.

A word that comes to my mind is homeostasis. It is the first stage within the wound-healing process. It's in this stage where the bleeding is stopped to keep blood within a damaged blood vessel from hemorrhaging. A hemorrhage means the blood vessel is leaking internally or externally. Many of us are bleeding on the inside because of what they said or did today, yesterday or maybe even years ago. Not properly handling the wound could lead to further damage.

The healing of a wound is very complex especially when dealing with a fragile heart. There is a process the body takes to repair itself in order to function again after being wounded. We can disregard the process but it doesn't prohibit the outcome. The wound-healing process consists of several stages that I believe will help us gain a deeper understanding in relation to forgiveness. Being unforgiving can prolong restoration so these steps are vital for recovery.

The first stage we touched on was homeostasis. The second stage is inflammation, the third is proliferation, and last being maturation. Each stage is required in order for healing to occur. Time is the most important factor in this equation. Let's not approach our hurting hearts with a quick fix. Some of this pain took years to get in so it may take a while to get out. We must first admit we are hurt and we want to be healed.

In the inflammation stage damaged and dead blood cells are cleared out, along with any debris. There are some relationships you will have to disconnect from in order to heal. There are some phone calls you cannot accept. You may have to disconnect from your world of clutter, associates, relatives and refuse to engage in wasteful conversations. You are in the inflammation phase of your wound. This means you are discarding the old and preparing a way for the new in your life. I believe this is one of the most difficult phases. This is the phase where change begins, and accepting change can be difficult after being accustomed to bleeding.

Whenever there is transformation involved we have a tendency of creating excuses. Excuses have never prevented a wound from bleeding. If anything, excuses only prolong the process and produce a series of infections. I have been a victim of allowing the hurtful words of others to cling to my mind like an unwanted parasite. In doing that, my mind became the host in which their words inhabited and infected the way I viewed my identity. I was never more vulnerable then in my wounded stage. There was a point when I became sick and tired of allowing bitterness and resentment to dictate how I lived and loved people. My frustration led to my falling to me knees and believing first that God had forgiven me. Being consumed by my own guilt made it difficult to forgive others. I finally got up off of my knees and was determined to no longer live as the host. Nothing forces you to accept change like being mentally, physically and spiritually exhausted with your position in life.

A parasite's only objective is to cling to the host for benefits. Unlike a predator, a parasite doesn't usually kill it's host. These people just want to live off you for an extended amount of time. Another group I would like you to be aware of is pathogens. This word stems from the Greek word *pathos* (suffering) and *genes* (producer of). It's bad enough you are trying to heal from hurt. The infirmities of life have already confined you to your bed. Then along comes another subtle attack reminding you that you were wounded and would love for your bleeding to continue. Your environment and the company you keep is so critical in the inflammation phase.

From my personal experience, I would encourage you to surround yourself with individuals who are producers of life, faith, joy, patience, peace, gentleness, endurance and most of all love. After all, you are so close to being made whole. Your breakthrough is directly connected to what you allow to enter and exit your life. Most importantly, I need you to know God loves you no matter how infectious the wound may look or feel.

I believe the most destructive force in our world is an unforgiving heart. I also believe the most powerful force in our world is forgiveness. Eventually the bleeding will subside and you will realize the pain is only temporary. Expressing forgiveness demonstrates another level of humility and maturity. It's in the stage of proliferation where the wound is being rebuilt. This is usually done at a rapid speed. Like I stated your environment is so essential to your recovery. Even your diet will have to change in order to heal properly. I have seen people develop poor eating habits, drug addictions, sexual addictions, and chronic illnesses linked to unforgiving.

Now that we have entered the growth phase of your wound, things are starting to feel normal again. You need to be closely monitored by accountable loved ones. In this phase I remember intentionally setting time aside to cry out to God, to sit quietly, scream if need be, and pray continually. I found a new outlet to clear my mind. The bleeding had ceased, the clutter was cleared and I sensed growth taking place in my entire being. There was a point where I was not eating properly and now I was in the phase where I started to regain my regular appetite back. It wasn't just the appetite for food. It was the appetite for being made whole. The people I began to surround myself with put a demand on my maturation. Their words of affirmation became the nutrients I needed to sustain my mind as it was being remodeled. Anything that would bring a deficiency to my time in prayer, exercise, or healthy eating was deleted.

Immediately after my heart begin to strengthen there were other individuals who had suffered from similar scrapes, bruises, relationship separations, heart breaks, cuts, and lacerations. The most valuable thing I learned while healing, that my wound was intended to heal somebody else. It was never about me. The pain your wound may be causing is not even about you. It's a tough pill to swallow but trust me, you can forgive and experience its power right now. After all, the person you are choosing not to forgive is probably living their life, while you are harboring the bitterness in your heart rejecting the healing that comes with forgiveness.

# The Challenge

Write down four people you know that deserve your forgiveness. Pick up the phone to call or text them. You may be thinking Jamel you don't understand they crossed the line. It's not a matter of whether you were right or they were wrong. It's a matter of releasing them and releasing the power of forgiveness. After you speak with them write down exactly how you felt afterward.

Names:
1.

2.

3.

4.


Feelings:
1.

2.

3.

4.


Ephesians chapter 4 verses 31-32 *³¹Get rid of all bitterness, rage, anger, harsh words, and slander, as well as all types of evil behavior. ³²Instead, be kind to each other, tenderhearted, forgiving one another, just as God through Christ has forgiven you.*

# SELF REFLECTION

# Chapter 9 Tweet That!

Learning, knowing, and understanding your lineage gives you foundation, identity, and direction.

The more you're around MEANINGFUL information the less time you spend in MEANINGLESS discussions.

For some people YOU'RE WELCOME and THANK YOU satisfies their hunger.

Fear grows in comfortability. Faith matures in discomfort.

God has placed His spirit inside the interior of your heart. To identify and understand people's ulterior motives - use discretion!

There comes a point where you have to want it for yourself and not because you're being asked to.

Scapegoating is a spirit. You don't have to except their wrong but you do have to confess yours.

If you are not ABLE don't RESPOND. Changing the world is a RESPONSIBILITY.

The purpose always outweighs the decision to quit.

There comes a point where you have to stop searching and start trusting.

God's love is unfailing even after we have fallen.

Touching the surface is good but getting to the root is better.

If we focus on what's fading we will miss what's being revealed. Both are important but only one has eternity attached to it.

Remember God has planted you in the middle of the chaos to be the order.

Surround yourself with people who will not step on your seed but give you moisture. They will not choke your belief, but believe your good soil.

There are two types of be done. It is and it will. Live in and speak the IT IS.

Don't allow their drama to cause you to make dramatic decisions. Your NO needs NO explanation.

Your life has already been pre-written by God. You're not obligated to respond to every casting call. #playyourpart

Make an effort to surround your purpose around your life and not your life around your purpose. It's in your purpose you find life.

Whether right or wrong. Signs are given/displayed to be acknowledged not ignored.

Identifying your weaknesses doesn't make you weak. It allows you to reveal your strengths.

There is your time and then the proper time. Trust that God owns the proper time.

Submission produces authentic humility that says I don't have it, I need help, and the hypocrisy must end now!

Whatever you are spiritually is what you will attract naturally.

It doesn't matter HOW it looks. What matters is who is with you in the HOW.

Your transparency and testimony is the light to someone's life.

Some people wait for you to fall to say I told you so! When we think God is not there He picks us up and says I TOLD YOU SO.

When they highlight your flaws more than they congratulate your progress. That's when you know it's time to distance yourself.

Your fate is not determined by the figures you make. And your faith is not released by you figuring it out.

Stop letting people who don't know who they are tell you who you are.

Asking for help does not make you a coward. It makes you a person that needs help.

Trust God knows how to deal with injustice, because He's INjustice and IN control.

What you tune into you will turn into.

WOW - Worship OVER Worry

There is always a purpose behind a pause. Just make sure you're prepared when the play button is pressed.

Admitting you're ignorant about a subject is better than pretending to know and fail.

God is using every intricate part of your life to shape your future. Don't force your way in. A masterpiece is never rushed.

Staying in an unhealthy relationship is like being buried alive. Eventually someone's going to run out of air.

Just because it tastes good doesn't mean it's not poison.

Sacrificing your character for the sake of having freedom is not freedom, it's an upgraded PRISON.

Scattered visions with good intentions create a team with excuses making bad decisions.

A person who has been esteemed and valued develops an open heart that is more receptive to encouraging words.

We have to be careful not to allow our wisdom to become prideful in the presence of ignorance.

Concepts are the source of communication and determines the success of our understanding.

Sometimes living casual leaves casualties. Accountability speaks high volumes.

Learn to distract the distractions with focused actions.

Most peoples opinions are given based on fears that have developed in their own lives. Fears' only objective is to stagnate the vision.

Overcoming allows you to achieve with ease. It's overcome then achieve not achieve then overcome.

Achieving continues to reach but never grabs its destiny. There is a difference between achieving and achievement.

# SELF REFLECTION

# Chapter 10 Obvious Faith

One day as I was driving down the road I stopped at a light. While sitting there I observed a man walking along the sidewalk wearing dark shades tapping his cane left to right. Through my observation I could tell he was visually-impaired. The first thought that crossed my mind was, I wondered what happen to him? I'm not sure what caused the defect in his sight. Whether it was a stroke, some sort of trauma, glaucoma or maybe just age-related. Either way, the image of him walking along the sidewalk begin to speak to me. Nothing increases your dependency on your ears like losing your sight. Then I begin to think about my faith. It was obvious he needed his ears to navigate down the road. I'm sure he had to develop a keen sense of hearing to prevent his feet from stumbling.

Dealing with relationships will require an impeccable amount of faith. Especially when we are talking about trusting God with our lives. I personally believe a relationship with God is the most important relationship. This doesn't mean we will not stumble. There had to be numerous times the visually impaired man fell. He had to experience several falls during his time of blindness. Through time, the keen hearing he developed probably decreased the amount of falls. The Bible states in Hebrews chapter 11 verse 1 *¹Now faith is the substance of things hoped for, the evidence of things not seen.*

The key word I would like to point out in this sentence is evidence. Evidence is defined as the available body of facts or information indicating whether a belief or proposition is true or valid. Therefore it is impossible to have faith in the unseen if you're relying on your sight. Faith is the substance which has supplied the fuel for every relationship I have encountered.

Like the blind man, I had to learn to see with my ears. I decided to weave his disability into my spiritual life. It was obvious the man was blind by simple observation. I thought to myself, how could I take my trust in God to another level? To the point where my hearing became so clear, I would literally make decisions based on what I heard. This didn't necessarily mean my hearing was more keen than individuals who depended on physical sight. Although, when you rely on your hearing to navigate, it changes the way you walk. Not only does your hearing and walking change after this adjustment, you will find the way you communicate is altered in a major way. The Bible states that faith is the substance of things hoped for, the evidence of things not seen. When your focus is on the unseen you speak with a lot more authority.

Your language shifts from "worry" to "it will occur". You go from being unsure to being confident. I've gotten to the point where I know longer need to ask a person what their faith is in. I totally believe you are going to have faith in someone or something.

By definition, obvious is something that is easily perceived or understood; clear, self-evident, or apparent. It's faith that produces the obvious. The key word projected from each definition is the word evident. When something is evident there is no need to ask what's happening. What was once in the unseen has appeared.

In my early teenage years I was a huge fan of several alcoholic beverages. The alcohol soon became my coping mechanism to suppress the world I lived in. Every challenge deserved its personal trip to the bar stool. I had so much hope that the bottles would take away the pain I even gave them nicknames. My E&J was easy Jesus, and Hennessey was Hen Roc. Of course there were many others depending on the type of pain I was experiencing. My faith in these beverages grew to a point where I valued them more than physical relationships. I had faith that the bottle would ease the stress. I believed a couple shots would clear my thoughts and iron out all my issues. It was all an illusion in my head. This illusion soon lead to heated arguments with friends and family. I had built my faith to a level where I begin drinking excessively.

One day as I was going in for my regular physical check up, the doctor said he noticed from a previous blood sample that alcohol was beginning to take a toll on my body. It was nothing life-threatening, but he advised me to discontinue drinking. It was clear and obvious to him I had built a psychological dependence on my drinks. He didn't really need to ask was I drinking. It was obvious where my faith was based on my blood results. My faith had produced the obvious.

The young lady walking down the street whose stomach is protruding does not need to be asked if she's pregnant. It's obvious she had faith in someone that produced a child in her womb. The communities that surround us filled with crime, poverty and social injustice suffer from problems that have become obvious. Relationships experiencing trials and triumph are clearly a result of where their faith was placed. Faith will always produce the obvious. I'm no longer spending countless hours discussing the obvious. We need to inject this same philosophy into our relationships. It's going to require a stupendous amount of faith and endurance to grow together through the storms of life.

James chapter 1 verses 2-4 *²Consider it pure joy, my brothers and sisters, whenever you face trials of many kinds, ³because you know that the testing of your faith produces perseverance. ⁴Let perseverance finish its work so that you may be mature and complete, not lacking anything.*

A lot of us have faith in our head, but it's the fire that places it in our hearts. Faith is one of the key components in the value of a relationship. When there is a trial in your marriage, when the finances are low, when the company sales are plummeting, and things become so clear it's obvious, it is during these moments there is no need to focus on the surface of the issue. Let's look at the faith root. Now that it's obvious the marriage is under pressure, money is low, and sales have declined. What are you going to do? We can choose to stay stuck in the obvious pointing fingers at each other, or take a step back and check our faith. It's going to require a certain level of faith to see a successful marriage while enduring the pitfalls of a crumbling marriage. It's going to require some tenacity to face economic decline. It's going to take skillful ingenuity to survive the retail drought.

The writer James says when, not if your faith is tested your endurance has a chance to grow. Then he goes on to to say, let it grow! I currently have the opportunity to manage a beauty supply store and a well-known inspirational clothing brand. I'm constantly in circles with very prestigious business men and women holding meetings about the potential of their company's future. The question people constantly ask is, "Don't you want the business to make a lot of money?" My reply would always be a simple word like, "Sure".

However, one day while I was inside of our beauty shop it hit me. After having a challenging year and feeling as if my endurance went bald, I had to consider it an opportunity for great joy and realize my faith was being tested so my endurance would grow. While pacing back and forth in the shop the spirit of God spoke to me. Why are you focusing on the obvious? After that moment I began to research the word obvious and I connected it to my faith in relationships. It's obvious you started a company in hopes to make a certain amount of revenue to sustain your family, save for retirement or perhaps plans to travel, or feed the hungry. Something that is apparent does not need as much attention, as what caused the manifestation. I shifted my paradigm from focusing on the obvious to focusing on the unseen. I began to spend less time talking and more time doing.

It's behind the scenes where the real creativity takes place. It's in the quiet place where the minister does most of his praying in preparation for the battle ahead. It's in the car where the homeless motivational speaker slept while crafting his most prolific speeches. It's behind bars where Nelson Mandela wrote his most inspirational poems to sustain him for twenty-seven years in prison. It's serving at the restaurant busing tables that allowed David Shands to script one of the greatest entrepreneur books titled *"Dreams Are Built Overnight"*. It was in the losing of her hair that prompted Madam C. J. Walker to develop some of the most outstanding hair care remedies that have existed. It was in the shoes of six-year old Ruby Bridges that traveled for miles determined to attend an all-white elementary school to put an end to segregation. It was in the genes of Albert Einstein, an absent-minded scientist who gave us the theory of relativity. It was in Moses on the top of Mount Sinai who delivered the ten commandments.

These prestigious men and women suffered behind the scenes. They had the fortitude to take the unseen by faith, and make it evident. Today we now study and admire what is obvious to everyone. The poems of Mandela, the entrepreneurial brilliance of Mr. Shands, the hair products of Madam Walker, the school integration of Ruby, the $E=mc^2$ of Einstein and the commandments of Moses. Although they have blessed us with such glorious benefits and we celebrate their ideas and persistence, it's through time that the obvious becomes oblivious. We remember, but we don't give as much attention to what's now apparent. I believe the true value is found in the unseen. So it's there we must continue to visit to be inspired over and over again.

Often, we choose to value a relationship when it's beneficial for us. The value is not always based on what you can see. In most relationships, especially between couples, there are some characteristics that are not revealed in the beginning stages. As time passes people are always evolving. Life is always testing the validity of the relationship collectively and individually. Chances are, the person you dated six months ago will not be the same person in terms of characteristics six years later. Progression is a wonderful sight to watch unfold.

During my ten years of being married I have watched my wife progress from a young nineteen-year old girl into a grown women and mother. The characteristics she displays now are not what she displayed when she was married ten years ago. I believe the hidden potential was always inside of her. Our marriage relied on having the capability to live in the unseen in order to endure every obstacle. It's obvious now that our marriage is amazing. Even when we fought, disputed, separated, and nearly divorced my value was in the unseen. I knew my marriage was predestined for greatness. I knew if I placed more faith in ending versus starting, forgiving, loving, and enduring it would be simple to throw in the towel. Now I spend more time focusing on what's being revealed in our relationship rather than what's fading. I'm aware that we may have a disagreement.

Now instead of focusing on the obvious, in the middle of the disagreement I'm tapping into how did the disagreement begin. I'm convinced there is no way the disagreement can last forever. If I am persistent about having faith in every situation, then peace, love, and joy will enter the disagreement and eventually the disagreement has to fade. In no way will I ignore that the disagreement did not take place. It's just that I have conditioned my mind to stay focused on faith to produce the results I desire in our relationship. I believe we lose sight of a person's true value through selfishness. When in fact, selflessness strengthens your focus to see what's being revealed.

# SELF REFLECTION

# Chapter 11 Finding Success In Serving

I believe serving is one of the most influential acts used to portray humility. Concealed in the heart of every servant, is a spirit of submission. We need to be careful not to confuse humility with being feeble, or submission with being a pushover. Nothing pleases me more than having the ability to serve people. It's in the midst of serving that I find the authentic value confined in the heart of mankind. I believe the most preeminent people are those who choose to value others over themselves. Selfless acts are not taught inside a text book and they cannot be learned in the corridors of your prestigious educational systems. Servitude and submission are developed in the institution of life experiences, which produces humility. Forced humility is considered humiliation.

When we speak of success, it can be defined in so many ways depending on the interpreter. When we speak of finding success, a majority of us lose sight of what success means to us. We redefine our belief system for a temporary gratification. Serving is so intertwined with value. The willingness to serve produces a giving mentality that values someone or something so much we feel obligated to give. Remember, valuable people attract people of value. The serving and giving system was set in motion way before we arrived on this earth. This system was in the mind of the creator delivered to mankind for our benefit. The book of Genesis starts with these ten words, "In the beginning God created the heavens and the earth." So, before anybody presented a definition of serving or success, God served us his masterpiece called earth, and he continues to define the purpose of what he served and the success it would bring.

When we want to find something, it gives the connotation of searching. Searching implies we want something that is lost which will benefit us when we find it. Think about the male reproductive sperm cell. Sperm stems from the Greek word *sperma* which means seed. A sperm cell is not just swimming to swim. These cells packed with twenty-three chromosomes are on a serving mission. Their main objective is to create a union between themselves and the female's egg. This astonishing act of giving usually takes place in a successful hallway titled the fallopian tube. It's here that fertilization transpires and submission is observed by one seed reaching it's destination. Sadly, everybody doesn't get to experience the luxury of this success. Whenever one sperm has entered the egg, the tail and the outer coating of the sperm disintegrate and a reaction takes place preventing other sperm from fertilizing the same egg. This is one of the most impeccable images of the value of relationship. This was God serving us to each other in order to continue production of mankind.

If we take the focus off of us we can see serving taking place all around us. The bees are serving the flowers through pollination. It's in the pollinating of flowers and other crops that enhances our agricultural industries such as nuts, berries, fruit and vegetables. The flowers are serving the bees through supplying pollen and nectar to produce strong colonies. The flowers provide a powerful source of carbohydrates from their nectar and protein from their pollen. This serving dependency displays one of the most powerful ecological interactions between two organisms. We may want to devalue the relationship between the bee and the flower, but they are a necessity to us just as much as we are to them.

Whether it is the sperm racing to fertilize the females' egg, the bees gathering pollen or the flower offering it's nectar, each species exhibits a sign of submission. Submission is defined as an act of submitting to the authority or control of another. Not every servant has the attributes of submission. Regardless of who you are, these characteristics were not wired into our DNA. Just because your father was a servant doesn't automatically make you a servant. Just because your mother loved to give doesn't mean you will love to give. Serving is not a trait that is inherited through genetics. Although it is not hereditary it can be deposited and developed.

I believe the Bible paints a vivid picture of finding success in serving by taking a glimpse into the life of Joseph, a young teenage boy who was serving his brothers by tending to their flocks. In the life of Joseph we can witness submission and serving being sculpted into his image through various trials. Joseph's life takes a drastic turn soon after telling his brothers about a dream that involved him reigning over them. The Bible says that they hated him soon after he shared his dream. Joseph then begin to share every dream with his brothers. You would think he would have ceased sharing his dream with them after their jealousy and rage over the first dream. His dreams became the fuel that drove his brothers to throw him into a pit and sell him into slavery for a few pieces of silver. He went from being a slave to living in the home of the Egyptian master. Genesis chapter 39 verse 2-4 states *²The Lord was with Joseph so that he prospered, and he lived in the house of his Egyptian master. ³When his master saw that the Lord was with him and that the*

*Lord gave him success in everything he did. ⁴And Joseph found favor in his eyes and became his attendant. Potiphar put him in charge of his household, and he entrusted to his care everything he owned.*

One thing Joseph recognized was the Lord was with him. Buried inside the dreams of Joseph was his success. Little did he know this success would require serving in unfavorable situations. Finding success in serving may lead to you being falsely accused, betrayed by love ones, serving a prison sentence, rejected, and labeled as the underdog. Potiphar's wife soon became attracted to Joseph and she accused him of trying to sleep with her. Her false accusations lead to Joseph being thrown in prison. While in prison, the Lord was with Joseph and showed him favor in the eyes of the warden. The warden soon placed Joseph in charge of the prison. Prison may seem like an unsuccessful place, but some of the greatest dreams and visions were birthed when there wasn't enough.

Maybe you are in a relationship that feels like a prison you didn't deserve. Trust me, the Lord can give you favor in that unfavorable situation. While in prison, Joseph is summoned to interpret a dream of the Pharaoh. His capability to interpret Pharaoh's dream and save Egypt from a famine took his success to another level. In return Pharaoh gives Joseph charge over the entire land of Egypt. He went from serving his brothers to serving an entire country. I found that there is a level in serving where you have just as much input as the owner. Everybody wants to be Pharaoh, but there are only a few willing to serve.

# SELF REFLECTION

# Chapter 12 Be Mindful

You cannot value someone else if you don't value yourself. I found when you value yourself, it's a lot easier to value others. One day as I was driving on the highway rushing to get to a meeting, I found myself ignoring the speed limit. As I was attempting to switch lanes I nearly ran into another vehicle. The car I was driving didn't have a blind spot detector. Due to my speeding, my position in his blind spot could not be observed under these conditions. Although an experienced driver could create the same situation while driving, my speeding only presented a higher risk of me colliding with another vehicle. Unfortunately I did not make it to my meeting any earlier. I got there just in time to receive a text message from my friend stating he was running fifteen minutes behind.

I'm sure we all have found ourselves speeding through life hoping that we could arrive a little sooner if we take a short cut. Maybe we could delay the pain of arriving behind schedule. Perhaps you have been rushing a relationship in hopes it would speed up the tempo of the process which seems like it has been sedated with a tranquilizer filled of stagnation. A relationship where you sense the proper adjustments should have been made to meet your needs. In most cases the problem is not visible when we are rushing or being driven by our emotions. The aspiration to obtain what we want disregards the care for others and being mindful is the last thing we consider.

Any relationship in which you intend to be mindful means that you are making a conscious effort to not abort the feelings of others. Not only does this apply in relationships, but it applies to all areas of our lives. I wasn't being mindful of the other drivers on the road as I was racing to my meeting. My carelessness endangered the lives of innocent commuters. Properly preparing for my day could have prevented me from swerving. Perhaps my thoughts could have been more centered. The urgency to do or say something occasionally produces premature results.

As a parent there are situations I have to contemplate prior to making a final decision. Making an irrational decision could potentially place my kids in danger or affect their future. Their interest has become more important to me versus my own. The way I respond a majority of the time will determine how they react. Not only have I made being mindful a chief principal in my family, I have made it a standard in all areas of my life. There are times when my actions are not in alignment with my thoughts and I noticed premature results being birthed. Fruitless words that have spewed out of my mouth without placing my feet in the shoes of the recipient. Businesses have collapsed from CEO's focusing on themselves and ignoring employee's input that may have given the company more outlets into the market and increased profits. Maybe you have avoided the feelings of people around you by becoming self-absorbed with your own feelings. Being mindful gives us the opportunity to readjust our value system and place people and situations in a better perspective.

Romans chapter 12 verse 2 *2Do not conform to the pattern of this world, but be transformed by the renewing of your mind.* It's in the mind where some of our toughest battles are fought. Our thoughts have the power to create a victorious life or one of being a victim. It's in the mind where our thoughts are processed, evaluated, and distributed. It's in the mind where emotions such as love, hate, fear and happiness are expressed. The mind has been associated with being part of the soul. The soul which consists of your mind, will and emotions.

The scripture above states we need to be transformed by the renewing of our minds. The Greek word for soul is *psyche* where we get our English word psychological or psychology. Psychology has to do with the study of the human mind and its functions especially those that affect our behavior. The challenge to progression involves refusing to change our state of mind. Nothing prevents or stagnates growth like a confused mind.

In order to be transformed it's going to require a new mind. Transform stems from the Greek word *metamorphoo* where we get our English word metamorphosis. Metamorphosis has to do with the complete change of the organism's appearance. The mind is the first step to experiencing a metamorphosis. Be careful, you may have to shut yourself in from the rest of the world.

We can learn a great lesson by looking at the life of a caterpillar. A caterpillar spends most of the early stages of their lives crawling around devouring food. When it's time to become an adult they begin to distance themselves from what they've been eating. The caterpillar has to be mindful of the next decision it makes. The next step is finding a safe place to pupate or begin their transformation into an adult. The caterpillar goes through metamorphosis by encapsulating itself in a cocoon. You may need to distance yourself from what you've been accustomed to eating, watching, listening to, and hanging around in order to go to the next level. It's not going to be painless or easy. You are about to undergo a total renovation. It's inside this cocoon, it's inside your safe place, where the complete makeover is occurring. This entire makeover involves you conducting an internal interview. This requires you sitting down in a quiet place and asking yourself some serious questions which regard you moving forward. Externally it looks like you have cocooned yourself into your own personal shelter away from all relationships. Internally there is a deep psychological renewal taking place. Your mind is being renovated, your will is being converted, and your emotions are being strengthened. The beautiful butterfly we admire flapping it's wings in the summer breeze did not just appear without going through a gruesome process. Most people ignore during the process and find it difficult to identify you when you come out of it.

Because of this decision we don't evaluate people by what they have or how they look. We looked at the Messiah that way once and got it all wrong, as you know. We certainly don't look at him that way anymore. Now we look inside, and what we see is that anyone united with the Messiah gets a fresh start, is created new. The old life is gone; a new life burgeons! Look at it! All this comes from the God who settled the relationship between us and him, and then called us to settle our relationships with each other.

# SELF REFLECTION

# Chapter 13 Word is Bond

The willingness to proceed even after the hardship you encountered, determines what you value sincerely. Growing up in the streets of New York, the phrase most noticeable to me was "your word is your bond". Your street credibility would be validated by what came out of your mouth. Your word was connected to your authenticity whether you believed it or not. A bond by definition is something that holds things together, a firm assurance, a covenant or seals the deal.

I remember being a teenager on the corner telling my friends my word is my bond. It became a cliché phrase that was spewed out of the mouth of most teenagers in my neighborhood. As the conditions and relationships in my neighborhood changed my words became less impulsive and more cognitive. I began to feel that me speaking out of haste without evaluating my thoughts devalued my character. This reduced the meaningless conversations I would have about promises I could not keep. This paradigm shift began to grow and fortify my relationships over the years. Now, when I tell someone I love you, I mean every letter and every word. The streets taught me how to mean what you say and say what you mean. There was one thing that always followed the word you spoke in the streets. There was no way of fleeing the test that proceeded what you spoke into the atmosphere. Your feelings were never factored into the equation. Either you were tested by the crowd you spoke in front of, or life was bringing opposition to your door step. The fact that you opened your mouth was a clear invitation for life to provoke you. You have two options after the test. You can either accelerate in what you believe or stand in an idle position reliving the situation your words spoke into existence.

The idea of remaining idle doesn't produce anything in our lives. Stagnation means you have decided to be motionless. In many relationships people can grow weary and lose motivation by false promises. When a person develops a form of apathy, the communication in the relationship begins to be slowly undermined.

I'm sure we can all agree that we have not kept our word in many situations. The husband who promised his wife they would have more kids as soon as he received a pay raise. The wife who assured her husband they could purchase the boat once all the debt was cleared. The company who guaranteed a promotion or the young man who said he would take care of the child. The politician that swore he/she would speak on behalf of the people or perhaps the leader who took an oath to serve God with all his heart.

In most cases the deal was never sealed because the word was faulty. In midst of making an oral declaration the covenant was broken. Sometimes the pressure of life can force you to speak without processing what it is you're saying, like the impulsive responses I gave as a teenager in my neighborhood. These type of responses only amounted to losing trust from friends, and not even trusting myself with what I was saying. Words have the power to destroy or build. They can shape your future into a master piece of love, peace, laughter and growth or create a canvas of pain, worry, doubt and fear. A dear friend of mine told me that you paint your world with your words. When I think of painting, it is such a creative expression. There are many styles of painting that express different meanings. I found it interesting that painting has something called color and tone. They are extremely important to painting just as pitch and rhythm are to music. We can often determine the value of the relationship based on the tone someone uses with you. For instance, there is no need for me to yell at you to get my point across. Your word is bond whether it is spoken softly in the valley or proclaimed aloud from the mountain top. Take a moment and imagine your words painting a picture in the relationships you're connected to. Now that you have the images in your head, ask your self a few questions.

What does my world resemble?

Does it resemble chaos and confusion?

How does my world affect my connections?

Are we being disconnected more than connected?

How does this painting affect the bond in my marriage, my friendships, my business and my relationship with God?

Are my words becoming less accountable?

Whatever your painting resembles, there is still time to make adjustments. No matter the color or tone of your life, God has the ability to give you a fresh canvas. Trust, he is much more than the allegory depicted in the Sistine Chapel. He is a true and living God that understands the power of words. He wants to equipt you with the tools to illustrate a firm and unmovable force.

Isaiah chapter 55 verse 11 *[11]It is the same with my word. I send it out, and it always produces fruit. It will accomplish all I want it to, and it will prosper everywhere I send it.*

The prophet Isaiah is giving a declaration of what the spirit of God spoke to him. God is the only one whose word is never broken. You can bank on Him coming through every time. It states that He will send

His word out and it will always produce fruit. When someone's word is bond it will always produce fruit. Not all fruit is healthy for you. Fruit can be produced from negative and positive words. Unlike man, God will always produce fruit that is beneficial for the sustaining of life. In the book of Galatians chapter 5 verses 22-23 it states *²²But the Holy Spirit produces this kind of fruit in our lives: love, joy, peace, patience, kindness, goodness, faithfulness, ²³gentleness, and self-control. Depending on who delivers the word, will determine the type of fruit that is produced.*

Remember, a bond gives the illustration of something being held together. In the beginning God made us in His image and likeness. We were assembled by the words He spoke. It was His word that formed man from nothing into something. Genesis chapter 1 verse 26 states *²⁶And God said, Let us make man in our image, after our likeness.* It took the words of the creator to bond us. Most of us find it difficult believing God's word because we don't believe our own word. There is no accountability in our agreements so our words become wasteful. Your words are the most important factor in the value of a relationship preceding your actions. Isaiah was speaking supernaturally saying the word of God will accomplish what God wants it to do. Naturally we encounter obstacles that are contrary to what God spoke over our lives. We have the tendency to speak what we see and it becomes our bond.

For years as a young man I was bonded to words that produced fruit that was not ripe. There was no love, joy, peace, patience, kindness, goodness, faithfulness, gentleness or self control. Maybe you have been bonded by words that have held you captive to fruitless relationships. Perhaps the supernatural word of God has lost its validity in your life. This may be because you lost your accountability in the natural due to inconsistence belief. It's difficult to believe the word of God when we have been eating fruit of doubt, fear, and unbelief. I encourage you to believe again as God said his word will prosper everywhere he sends it. His word resides in you at all times. Being made in His image deals with attributes. Someone may have painted your world and convinced you that all hope is lost. They may have convinced you that your image is distorted and you are of poor quality.

I have written this book to remind you that you have the characteristics of the One who holds the entire universe together by His word. You have the properties of someone uniquely designed with the traits of a supernatural God. You have the ability to stand on His word and it will become the new bond in your life. As you begin to unravel your God-given attributes, your words will change. You will begin to set a standard in your life where you hold yourself liable for what is spoken into the atmosphere. The lethargic vocabulary that used to control your paint brush will be dismantled. Your relationship circles will resemble ripe fruit in the eyes of spectators. They will count on you because your word is bond.

I want to leave you with a confession for both of us to be accountable. Please repeat this after me. Dear Lord, forgive me for not believing your word. I will no longer be a slave to fear, doubt, hate, anger, unbelief, inconsistency or any attributes that are not of you. Holy Spirit teach me how to live a life that is pleasing to God. My life will produce the fruits of the spirit which consist of love, joy, peace, patience, kindness, goodness, faithfulness, gentleness or self control. I will guard my mind, heart, eyes and ears. My word is bond and I am accountable for what comes out my mouth. In the name of Jesus, amen.

# SELF REFLECTION

# Chapter 14 Love The Hell Out Of Them

In every relationship there will exist a time where the thought of giving up seems like the best option for peace. I personally believe if physical or verbal abuse is the norm in your relationship it may be a sign to exit. However, the willingness to stay will require another level of love. I'm convinced humanity's love is impossible to break the chains of a guarded heart.

In the chapter the "power of forgiveness" I spoke about how an unforgiving heart will result in damaged relationships. It would be asinine to assume your relationship will never experience hurt. Pain is inevitable in every relationship. Couples will cause pain to each other, your boss will let you down, your relatives will break your heart and you will even disappoint yourself. Pain causes a discomfort that nobody just invites with open arms. No sane person wakes up and says "I want to intentionally experience the agony of physical or mental pain".

There may be a few that accept pain when it arrives, because they have reaped the benefits that came from suffering. I applaud those who have the capability to view hurt as an opportunity to love deeper. I believe society and the church has deduced the love of God to a rare phenomenon. When in fact it's going to require the love of God to drive the Hell out of someone.

One of my favorite verses in the Bible dedicated to the entire world is John chapter 3 verse 16 *[16]For this is how God loved the world: He gave his one and only Son, so that everyone who believes in him will not perish but have eternal life*". This love derives from the Greek word *agape* meaning the highest form of love. This love has been extended to you and me even when we did not deserve it. Since a young man I have attempted to encase my mind around God's love. His love is indescribable, unimaginable, unfathomable, and most of all unfailing.

His love continued to pursue me even when I wasn't pursuing him. I wanted nothing to do with God, Jesus or anything involving the gospel. The only relationship I valued was my own and the hooligans I hung out with. I would constantly hear people speak about how much God loved me. They would tell me about how he wants to have a relationship with me. The list would be endless, coming from family and random people I would meet. Out of all these conversations I still did not sense this amazing love everyone was raving about.

It wasn't until one night, as I was taking my routine walk through the park. I walked through this park almost every night after hanging out in the streets all day. This is where I would walk to clear my thoughts. This particular evening I sat on the same bench with my liquor in a cup. I sat there thinking about my life and the nonsense I was involved in all day. Then I begin to think about the numerous conversations I had about God's love. I thought to myself, is His love real? Will I ever experience this passionate love? If He loves the whole world then why don't I have any?

The relationships I was surrounding myself with did not portray authentic love but I continued to spend time with them. It was on that park bench in Columbus Ohio that the love of God seized my heart. While my thoughts were rambling on I felt this overwhelming compassion running through my heart. It was not like the love you receive from a parent, relative, or even a friend. I instantly knew my heart was being restored by the love of God. It was from that moment I begin to feel my anger subsiding. It was from that moment my depression started to leave. It was in that moment regret, hate, insecurity, and fear begin to leave.

Before this encounter all of the things I was battling with became a public and private Hell for me. Hell has been described in religious views as place of wickedness. Even outside of religion, people view the term Hell as something that is evil, troublesome, dishonest, corrupt or something that produces horrible behavior.

Prior to my experience on that park bench I was experiencing a troublesome life. I had an eye-for-an-eye, tooth-for-a-tooth mentality. I was immune to everything the characteristics of Hell had to offer. This attitude of retaliation was my way of justifying my ignorance. However, the love of God restricted me from viewing people through my old perception. Now, the agape love became a substitute standing in place of any vengeance I thought someone needed to be compensated. It's His love that began to dig deep into my heart and uproot every corruptible seed. Slowly I begin to sense His presence progressing in my life. I begin to experience his love literally loving the anger, fear, lust, hatred and anything that gave the appearance of Hell out of me. In return He replaced it with His genuine love.

My experience with the love of Christ overshadowed all of my experimental moments in the world. My desire became to emulate His love toward mankind every opportunity I was given. I knew if He could love the Hell out of me, I could love the Hell out of anyone I encountered through his love. Expressing his love allows me to catapult every relationship I engage in. Whether these relationships are short term, long term or a brief interaction I made with a stranger, His love creates a covering that acknowledges the flaw, but doesn't use the flaw as a flashlight to highlight a persons weakness.

The Bible says in 1st Peter chapter 4 verse 8 *8Most important of all, continue to show deep love for each other, for love covers a multitude of sins.* It's in the depths of God's love that we discover the treasures within a person. Their external image is no match for the super natural power His love possesses. In the midst of being betrayed, lied upon, cheated, manipulated, hated, abandoned, and any other form of misfortune you experienced, His love never fails and will always continue to win despite how it looks. It would be easy for us to love someone who loves us back. The true power of His love is expressed when all Hell is breaking loose in your relationships and you dig into the depths of your spirit and choose to love. I'm convinced that humanity's love is incapable of being persistent in the face of constant adversity.

# SELF REFLECTION

# Chapter 15 Experience vs Experiment

Your attachment to what you want is the very thing detaching you from what you need. It's in your need that your wants are met. Needs are different from wants and wants are different from needs. As elementary as this statement may be, people struggle with these two words on a constant basis. Relationships are severed all the time out of the desperation to fulfill a want. Even after this fulfillment is met we still feel empty. God never intended us to travel through life feeling empty, and experimenting with the conditions of this world. His intentions from the beginning was for us to be a reflection of His image and value one another. He created every experience to be beneficial for us. Whenever I think about how His master plan works, His spirit always directs me back to the beginning. Every illustration points back to foundation.

In the book of Genesis, man is alone walking with God in the cool of the day. There are two great experiences that have allowed me to develop my thoughts on experience versus experiment. The Bible says in Genesis chapter 2 verse 7 *7Then the LORD God formed the man from the dust of the ground. He breathed the breath of life into the man's nostrils, and the man became a living person.* This was not an experiment to see if mixing dust and breathing into the mans nostrils would work. Let me write it this way. God formed man from the dust and then God breathed his experience into the man's nostrils, and the man began to experience life as a living person.

The second experience that shifted my paradigm continues in Genesis chapter 2 verse 22-24 *22So the LORD God caused the man to fall into a deep sleep. While the man slept, the LORD God took out one of the man's ribs and closed up the opening. Then the LORD God made a woman from the rib, and he brought her to the man. 23"At last!", the man exclaimed. "This one is bone from my bone, and flesh from my flesh! She will be called woman, because she was taken from 'man. 24That is why a man leaves his father and mother and is united to his wife, and they become one flesh.*

The man goes through a very dramatic experience. God has put him into a deep sleep and He takes a piece of him to form his mate called woman. This describes an experience the solidifies the value of a relationship between a man and a women. We need to destroy the philosophy of this culture advocating that men do not need women and women do not need men. Trust me beloved, she is a part of you just as much as you are a part of her.

Don't let anyone deceive you into believing God made a mistake with this procedure. He was not experimenting. It wasn't until mankind decided to trust the serpent's judgment of them. As the story continues we see in Genesis chapter 3 verse 4-7 *4You won't die!", the serpent replied to the woman. 5God knows that your eyes will be opened as soon as you eat it, and you will be like God, knowing both good and evil. 6The woman was convinced. She saw that the tree was beautiful and its fruit looked delicious, and she wanted the wisdom it would give her. So she took some of the fruit and ate it. Then she gave some to her husband, who was with her, and he ate it, too. 7At that moment their eyes were opened, and they suddenly felt shame at their nakedness. So they sewed fig leaves together to cover themselves.*

We find in the text above that they were deceived into thinking they needed to experiment with something outside of God's experience in order to be fulfilled. As soon as they traded the experience for an experiment their eyes were opened and they suddenly felt shame. How many times have you experimented with something you knew was no good for you and later felt shame? How many times did you say no, but tried it anyway and your eyes were opened later and you felt shame? Who or what is trying to persuade you to trade in your experience to experiment with something that will cause you to have to hide? Wherever you are in life the power of His experience that was blown into your nostrils carries enough grace to redeem you. It's in the experience that He supplies the need that contains your wants.

In Philippians chapter 4 verse 19 it states *19And this same God who takes care of me will supply all your needs from his glorious riches, which have been given to us in Christ Jesus.* From this statement when can clearly see that He wants to supply every need in conjunction with the experience given by Christ.

Before we move forward, I would like define experience and experiment. Experience is the fact or state of having been affected by or gained knowledge through direct observation or participation. An experiment is an operation or procedure carried out under controlled conditions in order to discover an unknown effect or law, to test or establish a hypothesis, or to illustrate a known law. Both of the words share a resemblance, but only through experience are the facts guaranteed before the process begins. Everybody does not share the same experiences in life, but we are all given the choice to experience a relationship with the creator of life. Based on what you select will determine where your value system is and what you experience. The world we live in offers plenty of alternatives outside of a life with God. A world that is designed to keep you trying to establish yourself absence of His presence, relying solely on your experiments.

There is still no logical reason of how I sustained the relationships I have in my life. I have been given the most amazing relationships one could ever ask for. Even in the midst of adversity, financial strains and obstacles, I'm convinced that my experience with Jesus sustains me and gives me victory every time. I remember asking my wife, what does God, confidence, and coincidence have in common? I would wait patiently for her to respond before revealing my answer. My reply would be, you can be confident God is not a coincidence.

My dear reader your life is not an accident, you are not an experiment that God decided to test, and you are far from a hypothesis of an unexplained phenomenon. God controls every condition and your life is predestined for greatness when you are connected to Him. I believe this world has powerful information to navigate us through life. On the contrary, I'm not convinced in any way that experimenting with false solutions will solve our relationship issues. When we disconnect ourselves from the source the only option left is to experiment.

In my teenage years I decided God was the last thing I needed in my life. I decided to live by my own prerogative. I traded in my experience with him and decided to experiment with the streets. I figured the void in my life could be filled with drugs. Eventually drugs became my daily experiment to comfort me while separated from the life-changing experience He had to offer. There were relationships in my life that extended His grace toward me, but I rejected them. In my adolescent mind the experience required a process that took too long. I needed results that were expedient. Experimenting with drugs, whether selling or using brought instantaneous fame and relief. The gratification of fast money and short term highs started to fade when I realized they never gave me the experience I desired. When my high left my peace left. When I sobered up my heart still hurt. When the car lost the new smell, the newly-furnished home became quiet. When the relationship took a drastic turn, the only thing remaining was a laboratory lifestyle filled with failed experiments.

I decided to trade in my personal theories for the theology of the Kingdom. Theology deals with the study of God and his nature. I believe God orchestrated every experience in my life to get me to this point. His experience is a guaranteed win despite how it looks externally. Nothing we face in life is a surprise to the author and finisher of it all. In the book of Jeremiah chapter 1 verse 5 it says *⁵I knew you before I formed you in your mother's womb. Before you were born I set you apart and appointed you as my prophet to the nations.*

I want to place emphasis on the writer saying God knew you before he formed you in your mother's womb. Before any parts of your embryo were developed you were experiencing the creator's hand upon you. Having his experience doesn't mean that you are infallible. His experience actually begins to strengthen your dependency in following His way. His experiences are designed to bring victory in your life. Whether minuscule or major, nothing compares to having a godly encounter invade your atmosphere. It's the godly encounters that have allowed me to increase production in my business, sustain a healthy marriage, raise my respectable children and the instinct to write this book. Plenty of entities have decided to separate themselves from this encounter for whatever reason they deem important. In the end, that is the power of choice. You get to choose your experience or experiment.

# SELF REFLECTION

# Chapter 16 Lose Your Life

A majority of our destruction stems from selfish ambitions. The truth is, deception exists only to convince us that division is the best option. This same division has paralyzed our understanding of individual and collective growth. Of course, there is nothing wrong with being ambitious. It's the act of being selfless that enhances our value. In order to really comprehend the value of relationships, it will require you to let go of something you consider valuable. Ambitions do not normally benefit others. There is a type of selflessness that brings you to the point where you are willing to give your last so someone else may experience their first. Immediately, I know your mind went straight into preservation mode. Giving up your last sounds like you are taking a loss. You are being placed in a position where the life you have is complete, and giving any of it away would mean you are incomplete. I'm sure there are certain words that begin to gnaw at your thoughts. Words like impaired, inadequate, needing, missing, lacking, deprived, without and the famous four words I always hear is, *"WHAT ABOUT MY STUFF?"*

Eventually these thoughts begin to create a heart of ungratefulness that is rooted in pride. I want you to pause, and carefully do an inventory assessment of what you have. That fact that you are reading and comprehending this book lets me know that you possess more than most. Your sensory organs are triggering certain nerves to organize and process this information within your brain. Perhaps you are blind and your fingers are skimming across the braille on the pages making recognition by touch. Now, these brief examples may seem minuscule and pointless depending on the recipient. The fact still remains. There is a lot for you to be grateful for. You are probably reading this book thinking what does losing my stuff, my life or giving up my way have to do with the value of relationships? My dear friend it has everything to do with it.

Once again, Jesus was one of the most impeccable speakers to ever walk the earth, and he told an amazing story about a rich fool. In Luke chapter 12 verses 14-21 Jesus replied, *14Friend, who made me a judge over you to decide such things as that?" 15Then he said, "Beware! Guard against every kind of greed. Life is not measured by how much you own." 16Then he told them a story: "A rich man had a fertile farm that produced fine crops. 17He said to himself, 'What should I do? I don't have room for all my crops. 18Then he said, 'I know! I'll tear down my barns and* build bigger ones. Then I'll have room enough to store all my wheat and other goods. *<sup>19</sup>And I'll sit back and say to myself, "My friend, you have enough stored away for years to come. Now take it easy! Eat, drink, and be merry!"* *<sup>20</sup>But God said to him, 'You fool! You will die this very night. Then who will get everything you worked for?'"* *<sup>21</sup>"This is how it will be with whoever stores up things for themselves but is not rich toward God."*

Yes, a person is a fool to store up earthly wealth but not have a rich relationship with God. Again, God is directing us back to the value of relationships. I believe he desires for us is to encounter abundance in every area of our lives. I don't believe he wants the riches to overtake us and consume our attention. This form of consumption has a tendency to remove our focus from the eternal source to temporary resources.

Sometimes we believe our lives are more important than the life God wants us to live. When you view life from a human point of view it will be difficult to give up your life. God wants us to view life through His eyes. He places emphasis all throughout the Bible the plans that He has for our lives in Him. In Jeremiah chapter 29 verse 11 God speaks through the prophet saying *<sup>11</sup>"For I know the plans I have for you,"* says the LORD. *"They are plans for good and not for disaster, to give you a future and a hope."*

The perspective in which you view life will determine your willingness to surrender. In Matthew chapter 16 verse 21-24 Jesus is speaking to his disciples. He challenges Peter who attempted to reprimand him for making a statement about Him having to suffer and being killed. From then on Jesus began to tell His disciples plainly that it was necessary for Him to go to Jerusalem, and that He would suffer many terrible things at the hands of the elders, the leading priests, and the teachers of religious law. He would be killed, but on the third day He would be raised from the dead.

But Peter took him aside and began to reprimand him for saying such things. *<sup>22</sup>"Heaven forbid, Lord,"* he said. *"This will never happen to you!"* *<sup>23</sup>Jesus turned to Peter and said, "Get away from me, Satan! You are a dangerous trap to me. You are seeing things merely from a human point of view, not from God's."* *<sup>24</sup>Then Jesus said to his disciples, "If any of you wants to be my follower, you must give up your own way, take up your cross, and follow me. If you try to hang on to your life, you will lose it. But if you give up your life for my sake, you will save it."*

In Matthew 10 it says *"If you cling to your life, you will lose it; but if you give up your life for me, you will find it".*

In both chapters Jesus is placing emphasis on offering up your life.

He first begins by informing His followers how He will suffer terrible things by the religious leaders. Then He continues by giving them a quick notification about being killed and rising from the dead on the third day.

Peter steps up boldly and tells Jesus this is not going to happen. Peter did not want Jesus to lose His life, but Peter was merely seeing things from a human's point of view and not God's. In life you will meet individuals who suffer from the Peter syndrome. They will try to scold you for deciding to start. From their view point it's better to live in your current life then to let it die. They will constantly try to persuade you that your way is the best way.

I spent years in the streets prior to accepting Jesus. I truly believed in my chaotic world I was living the life, when in actuality it was a mirage of the true life He desired for me. Jesus knew in order for mankind to experience gain He had to literally lose His life. In our human minds we have been conditioned to believe the more we gain the more we win. Jesus arrives on the scene with this new edition of addition, using subtraction as His new system of obtaining increase. Losing your life does not mean you have to physically die, although we all know death is inevitable. That is one destination that cannot be avoided by anyone. We all may have a desire to live forever, but unfortunately we all have an expiration date. Our time on earth is just a temporary stay in comparison to an eternal life. Not only our lives, but everything that exists has an expiration date. We have convinced ourselves that our possessions in life will not expire. This is no different from the story of the rich fool Jesus spoke about. He stored up all his earthly wealth over a rich relationship with God. In hindsight he was hoarding his life and possessions.

I recall staying at a friend's house a few years ago. We agreed that I would be staying for the summer until I relocated into a place of my own. One particular afternoon I had an appetite for something to snack on. Since we were close friends I got up off the sofa and went into the pantry to grab a few snacks. Now, there was a wide selection to choose from in this pantry. However, my eyes immediately became fixated on this box of crackers. Without any hesitation I asked if I could grab a few. The response I received was as if I reached inside of a lost treasure chest and touched a rare diamond. The tone was filled with resistance. Thinking my friend was being sarcastic I reached into the box. This is when the voice erupted with hostility. My friend stood behind the door with gritted teeth grunting "Do not touch any of my snacks". I still remember them eerie eyes gazing at me as if I stole something. This was a side of my friend that I had never seen before. For a few days my mind was confused and I was unsure in how to approach the situation. I didn't want to leave that summer with my heart feeling displaced from our family bond. Eventually we discussed why he felt this way. We managed to end our summer peacefully without any harsh feelings toward each other.

The following summer I came back to visit for a few weeks. One morning I woke up and made my way to the same pantry and lo and behold sitting on the shelf before me were the same delightful crackers. At first glance I recognized they were in the same spot. Instantly, I knew I was about to relive the same scenario again. This time around my friends reply was "Go for it, what's mines is yours". Reaching for the box I tore open the package, grabbed a few and begin to chew. Unfortunately, as I was chewing the crackers I noticed they were stale. Instantly in that moment I heard the voice of God speak to me. He said, "Now Jamel, nobody can enjoy them". He then continued to speak to me about my possessions and my life. The crackers were a form of hoarding or holding onto something to the point they had expired and were no longer beneficial to anyone. This scenario is a depiction of a life lesson. I learned that it was possible for a person to hoard their life. We consume our lives with meaningless meetings, thoughtless errands, false obligations, materialistic possessions and call ourselves busy. Often we are too busy to spend time on our real purpose, believing we will miss the temporary pleasures of life.

A large majority of people in our world are weighed down by circumstances that are uncontrollable. There are some circumstances you can manage and some that are designed to teach patience. It's in the uncontrollable situations that Jesus taught about life, money and possessions.

In Matthew chapter 6 verses 24-34, Jesus starts his message by telling the people, *24"No one can serve two masters. For you will hate one and love the other; you will be devoted to one and despise the other. You cannot serve God and be enslaved to money. 25That is why I tell you not to worry about everyday life-whether you have enough food and drink, or enough clothes to wear. Isn't life more than food, and your body more than clothing? 26Look at the birds. They don't plant or harvest or store food in barns, for your heavenly Father feeds them. And aren't you far more valuable to him than they are? 27Can all your worries add a single moment to your life? 28And why worry about your clothing? Look at the lilies of the field and how they grow. They don't work or make their clothing. 29Yet Solomon in all his glory was not dressed as beautifully as they are. ³⁰And if God cares so wonderfully for wildflowers that are here today and thrown into the fire tomorrow, he will certainly care for you. Why do you have so little faith? ³¹"So don't worry about these things, saying, 'What will we eat? What will we drink? What will we wear?' ³²These things dominate the thoughts of unbelievers, but your heavenly Father already knows all your needs. ³³Seek the Kingdom of God above all else, and live righteously, and he will give you everything you need. ³⁴"So don't worry about tomorrow, for tomorrow will bring its own worries. Today's trouble is enough for today."*

The statements that are made in the passages above are so profound. It's in these scriptures where you will find some of the key principles on how to the value relationships. How often do we worry about life and the things we have gathered? Humanity has continually tried and failed to do life without the creator of life. Outside of the life God has intended for all of us, is a life of worry, frustration, sorrow, doubt, anxiety, and many other unnecessary afflictions. If we're honest with ourselves nobody wants to give up their way. Our world is obsessed with instant gratification and temporary satisfaction that leaves us feeling empty in the end. I'm fully convinced it's impossible to value relationships and be immersed in our possessions. Remember you will either hate one and despise the other. It will also produce a life of worry. Our way is harder to break free from when were buried in worry. Valuing relationships and losing your life will not be painless, effortless, trouble-free or simple.

Yes. the process will be complicated but worth it in the end. This value is connected to generations to come. This type of value is the value Jesus saw when He was nailed to the cross. He saw you and I eventually having to give up our world in order to truly live. This is a daily crucification we are currently living. You and I have to die daily to our way in order to truly live. I believe by you reading this book faith will come alive in your heart. That faith will give you the ability to surrender your life, break the addiction, leave the hurtful relationship, exit or start the company, forgive again, say it is finished and legitimately begin to value relationships.

# SELF REFLECTION

Made in the USA
Columbia, SC
02 September 2020

"The Value of Relationships is a great gathering of profound literature.

The book is a tool that can be used to enlighten and provoke healthier relation-ships amongst all walks of life, not just the bond of man and wife.

Jamel has written a book that should be given out in schools and workshops.

Great relationships lead to great oppurtunities. This book will help you navi-gate through your relation-ships wiser."

- Dj Fadelf

Jamel Dev'on Jackson (Author, Philanthro-pist, Community activist and Public Speak-er) has been teaching on the topic of Re-lationships for more than ten years. Jamel has spearheaded several business activa-tions surrounding the purpose of bridging the gap between families, streets, teenag-ers, public figures, and it's communities.

Mr. Jackson has spoken on a plethora of relationship panels, consulted, counseled, and transformed countless lives by his in depth understanding of the Value of Relationships. With over ten years experience on topics such as dating on purpose, saving sex until marriage, entrepreneurship, family res-toration and forgiveness. Mr. Jack is on a mission to inspire the world soul at a time. Be sure to indulge i Jamel's new book "The Value Of F tionships". A book that will enlighte your mind and lift your spirits.

ISBN 9781680920819

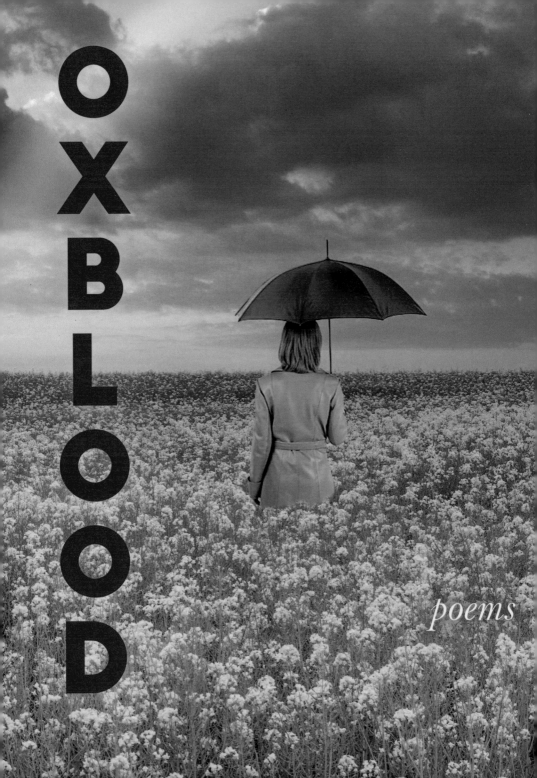

# OXBLOOD

*poems*

Nicole Caruso Garcia